MAMA LIKES MY COWLICK

MAMA LIKES MY COWLICK

Terry Powell

To order additional copies of this book, contact:
Xlibris Corporation
1-888-795-4274
www.Xlibris.com
Orders@Xlibris.com
105246

PROLOGUE

This is not my first offense against the literary profession. The first was a misdemeanor. This one is likely a felony. Out of respect for chronology, I recommend reading the misdemeanor first, but if this is the only one available, go ahead, commit the felony; let the hide go with the hair.

I sent the misdemeanor to a reluctant publisher on April Fools Day 2010. I thought it was fitting and proper to register the offense on that day. I was duly rewarded for my insight. The little booklet destroyed previous sales records, posting the least number of sales since Methuselah's publication, "A Brief History of Mankind." Methuselah's effort barely reached double digits, but it outsold mine. Apparently, no one was interested in Methuselah's little essay but a crazy old eccentric named Noah.

My gratitude goes out, however, to those few friends and family who were brave enough to read my first writing. Some reported that it gave them a tingly feeling, followed by twitches and ticks, then flinches and grimaces, ultimately producing a wave of nausea, and a desire to heave their insides in the direction of the author.

I suppose it is best that the world at large is sheltered from those sensations. When and if the world at large takes such a leap of faith, I am certain they will be as congratulatory toward their predecessors as I am. I remain fascinated with the patience they sacrificed to endure my writing.

I registered my first offense under the title, "Come Out, Come Out, Yo House Is On Fire." The title came from the ancient sport of "doodlebuggin" which is explained in my first writing for those deprived souls who did not grow up Southern. In addition, I expounded upon other fascinating events and people in that writing which would be beneficial to understanding this one. It is because of the sequential nature of the writings that the first chapter here is listed as chapter six.

I aptly entitled this one, "Gullible's Travels", the silly equivalent of Terry's Ramblings, until I discovered that Ring Lardner used up that title in 1917. I am yet to read his edition, but I intend to, some day.

I decided then to call it, "Just One Heart Beat From Hell", but that title was taken as well, I believe by a Christian rock group called The Staggers. So I will call it something reasonably original, when I think of it.

This writing chronicles what I commonly refer to as my cowboy years, from ages ten to fifteen. I had hoped to squeeze ten years into this writing, but it waxed fat and kicked, and busted out, and I am yet to hem it up. I could have written several books about that short but potent span of time. But, who really cares about my personal musings anyway, billions upon billions will never get wind of it, and most of the ones who do will turn their nose up at it and say to themselves: "what does he know."

A good friend once gave me some good advice which applies well to my desire to be an author. He said, "Terry, don't take yoself so seriously, nobody else does."

Someone asked me if this was a "tell all" book, to which I replied, "there is no such thing, outside the Bible." A man only tells what he wants told, and quite often it would be told differently if somebody else told it.

I am simply reminiscing the past as I remember it, and describing as best I can some of the events and people that made an impact on my life. There are some things none of us can tell without the benefit of a witness protection program.

Since I am not privy to all the pieces of the puzzle, even in my own life, some of it has to remain a mystery. I have learned over the years to grow quite comfortable with mystery, more specifically with the fact that I do not know everything; and quite frankly, that I do not necessarily need, or want to, know everything. People who think they know everything often try to teach me, but they always end up hopelessly frustrated and defeated when I ask them questions that even they cannot answer.

I see no need for me to apologize if my perspective of the past differs from yours, since none of us experience the exact events in exactly the same way. We all have some difficulty fully accepting each other's perspective.

Thanks for taking the time to read my writing, and if you find little value in it pass it on to someone with a greater flair for obscure literature. I believe there is a sizeable remnant of readers like me, still lurking about in the shadows, starving for that which rings true, pillaging through dark and dusty back room shelves, hungry for the rare and raw and unrevised versions of history.

CHAPTER 6

Come early evenings, mostly Thursdays after supper, after the livestock sale, I would weave my bicycle through the quarter mile of dried mud ruts, down Reid Street, down behind the old Pelham Tobacco Warehouse and her new little sister, Big Dixie; down behind the cotton gin; further on down to the lonely and obscure two acre lot where Mr. Gilmer stabled his mules. Hardly anybody ever went way down there more than once, but me, and Mr. Gilmer and Buddy Thomas.

There I would throw my bicycle down in the dirt, anxiously scale the northern wall of his old mule barn, knowing full well that the western wall leaned precariously against a stand of volunteer pines and pecans. I was almost always alone, except for Speck the canine terrorist. Like my father before me, I have always had an excessive urge for solitude.

Squirrellike, atop my eight foot perch, I would fold my arms over on the top rail, drop my chin down over them and scan the lot, eyeballing each animal, and studying them at length, lingering meditatively over each new addition to accurately evaluate the potential of Mr. Gilmer's latest investment.

My response was always the same: "damn, ain't nothin' but mules . . . mules and more mules . . . miles and miles of mules." I was recently ten years old, and I had learned to cuss to myself; not out loud mind you, for those who taught me had also taught me discretion. I logged a good bit of time back then as a closet cusser, perfecting the skill of my profane heroes.

I may have become the best private cusser in Pelham, Georgia had it not begun to leak out early and spill onto my mother who whipped me back into moderation. Even so, I held up my end of the hypocrisy for a good little while, a legitimate candidate for an Oscar. Not many of my friends could span the split in my personality—a teetotaler in public, but a creative graphic designer in private.

Mr. Gilmer's mules were slick and shiny, and stout and healthy when he sold'em, but often when he bought'em they were hairy, and scrawny, and weak and wormy. He kept a barn full in stock, all shades of bays and sorrels and greys. He held no prejudice for mule skin, but he couldn't tolerate one that wouldn't work. Those didn't hang around very long.

His mules roamed freely over his haggard two acre briar patch, scattering themselves out all over, pillaging, scavenging, nibbling around the rusty skeletons of ancient farm implements, twisting their flexible lips around random rolls of worn out fence wire and clumps of bricks from fallen chimneys.

Everything seemed to move slowly there . . . time just creeping along . . . each second dragging itself up to the next, like two slow and lazy men stacking feed sacks . . . just barely perpetuating . . . contented . . . moving just enough to stay alive.

I don't reckon you could call us friends, me and Mr. Gilmer. We hardly ever saw each other. I was always elsewhere, schoolin', playin' ball, workin', and ridin' Mr. Hoke's horses. Mr. Gilmer left early in the morning with his heaviest pair of mules sagging the timbers in his dilapidated old trailer. He returned at odd intervals with perishing clod hoppers, ready for the glue factory. Mr. Gilmer traded mules unlike anyone else—door to door.

Daddy Powell said that Mr. Gilmer was a good man, they had been neighbors years ago; he said that Mr. Gilmer knew every mule in Mitchell County by name. I wanted to know Mr. Gilmer, but time was not our friend.

I just happened by his place whenever I could with a faint and wild hope that he had traded for a new horse that I could ride, but I always carried with me the constant expectancy of his absence, and the absence of a novel horse.

One cold Saturday morning, cold enough to taste the frost in your breath, cold enough to enjoy sitting by the fire and sipping chicken noodle soup and nibbling soda crackers, I decided to mosey down to Mr. Gilmer's place and see what was up. Miraculously, his battered old truck and trailer were there, linked together as always. "What God hath joined together, no man can tear asunder".

I skidded my bike up against a fence post and trotted over and peeked in his tilted tin top shack, sandwiched there between the barn and the pasture. It appeared as if it had staggered further east since I last saw it, and now it leaned a little too much toward Railroad Street to suit me. Both front and back shotgun doors were standing wide open, their chains dangling through the holes that secured them through corresponding holes in the wall.

I wandered in slowly and cautiously and viewed the contents for the first time. He did not need the chains; there was nothing there worth stealing. It was a junk yard inside, stacked waist high throughout the place was old sweat dried harness, and tarnished bridles and bits, decreasing in value the deeper they lay in their decomposing piles.

Homemade hardware hung on the walls alongside collars with cobwebs undisturbed since the Great Depression. Musty and molding halters littered the place and rotting ropes of all shapes and sizes were scattered all about. On the shelf that ran around the top of the place was strange and bizarre mule doctoring instruments, gooey and greasy ointments, cans of purple medicine, mostly dried up, and a holocaust museum of flies.

The carpet was mule hair, wall to wall, loosely distributed, you could drag your foot and rake up a pile as the wharf rats had proudly discovered. The bowed pine floor was failing miserably at keeping the sandy dirt from squeezing up between the cracks and mingling with the mule hair.

Mr. Gilmer came in the back door zipping up his pants and glanced over at me nonchalantly. He got out nearly half a cigar and began to chew where he had already chewed a while. After a spell of studying my frosty face, he squinted a little, and the light in his eyes brightened, and he prophesied, "you Keesie's boy, ain't you, Uncle Tom's grandson." I felt alright then, because now we knew each other.

I said" yesser", and he grinned some, and I knew for sure then that we were friends at last.

He sat down in the only chair in the place, and took out his Barlow and started to whittle. I wandered 'round about some more, like I was in a dime store, until I had seen all there was in the place. Then, I stood there in the middle of the mess and began to study him. He didn't pay me no mind as he was content to chew and whittle and look off out the front door to some place far away from where we were.

I noticed that Mr. Gilmer wore his clothes loose, like he had bought them a long time back, when he was younger and stouter. He was aging now, his shoulders stooping some, his neck and face gaunt, and I saw that his old scruffy brogans were hungry and chewing up his silk grey socks; they had chewed them up so that his boney snow white ankles shined through like moonlight.

There was no moonlight in his hands, they were darkened, sun drenched, wrinkled, with puffy purplish-blue veins running down from his wrists and branching off into his lanky fingers. His eyes were humble and happy and made me glad we were friends at last.

I shivered as a cold burst of wind blew through the old shack from front to back, but Mr. Gilmer didn't seem to notice. I began to wonder where he got the heavy dose of contentment that seemed to soothe his rugged spirit. The silent minutes were slowly marching off with a rare, mystic morning until Mr. Gilmer said, "Lil' Keesie, you wanna ride?"

"A mule?" I asked.

"Nosser", he said, "I got myself a real hoss yesterdee . . . nearly stole'em."

"Yesser", I said, in disbelief. "I ride Mr. Hoke's horses for'em all the time . . . I reckon I can ride yors too."

Mr. Gilmer said, "I bet you ain't never rode no horse like I got . . . you ever rode a walkin' horse, Lil' Keesie . . . a Tennessee Walking Horse?"

"Nosser" I said, "ain't never rode one 'cause I ain't never seen one, but I'll ride it just the same." I was simultaneously and sufficiently ignorant and bold at ten years old; not a healthy mix, but relatively common in my experience.

Mr. Gilmer bent his Barlow back flat and hid it in his khakis, and he poked his chew back in his Prince Albert can and slid it back in his shirt pocket, snapping the pearly snap down over it. He leaned over a little and pressed hard on his knees, slowly pushing himself about half way up, giving the kinks in his back time to dismiss their rebellious notions; then, he eased on up straight and stretched out the rest of the rebels.

He walked over and fetched a fancy black bridle from the back of his truck. It was so lavishly studded with silver diamonds that my eyes began to sparkle as did my desire to ride this majestic new horse from Tennessee. I began to paint a picture in my mind of the beauty I was about to behold.

I followed Mr. Gilmer's footsteps to the barn gate where he unlatched the chain that secured the living room of a couple dozen of the finest mules in Mitchell County. The herd moved toward us in unison until they saw that Mr. Gilmer had no feed, just a fancy black bridle behind his back. Accustomed to disappointment, the mules balked and rolled their envious eyes upward into the rafters where the fat pigeons roosted and flew freely in and out the prison gates.

Mr. Gilmer let out his whistle, "whew-a-wheet", it went, followed by, "com' 'ear Sophie, com' 'ear girl." Out of that pack of prize mule flesh staggered the lean and ghostly shadow of what was once a horse, a Tennessee Walking Horse, I reluctantly reckoned.

She was poor as a stump preacher, matted with cuckle burrs and beggar lice, her long legs stiff and stove up, her boney head sagging and pitifully wagging side to side as she humbly ambled over.

She shore is a friendly old cuss, I thought, as she came right on up close and nudged her loose lips up against Mr. Gilmer's coat pocket. As he rubbed her under the chin and slipped a sugar cube in her mouth, I sensed that she already knew him as an easy man to love.

There was hardly enough horse in that ol' bag of bones to make a pony, I kept thinking . . . I bet her teeth are worn down to a nub, and she's way too tall and skinny. She looked like she had walked all the way here from Tennessee and was plum give out. I believe we would have a better ride if we saddle up one of them wharf rats over yonder in the shed.

But I didn't dare say none of this out loud, I was just thinking, and wondering if Sophie could ever make anything more than half a case of dog food. I couldn't see where Mr. Gilmer got the pride he had for ol' Sophie, but he held it just the same, I could see it in his eyes, he was proud of his new hoss, and he was not about to turn it loose no time soon. L'l Keesie, he said to me, "This here ain't no ordinary horse.

I was sorry now that I said I would ride. My youthful indiscretion had misdirected my courage, and it was melting into a pile of pity. I was afraid that Sophie would collapse in the red clay in middle of Reid Street under the weight of a shiny black diamond studded saddle and the cold hearted rump of a city cowboy.

I could visualize the picture on the front page of the Pelham Journal. There I am, like Satan himself, seated atop a poor bay mare that has already collapsed spraddle-legged on her belly, all fours headed in different directions, looking as if I had viciously forced out the final dusty breath of a gentle, aged lady.

But, in those days, the constitution was clear—whatever a man bit off was what he had to chew. I found myself precariously perched between the paradox of malicious behavior and this cardinal principal of manhood. Without any faith of my own, I looked to Mr. Gilmer who handed me his. Sometimes, second hand virtues are all we have to live by, but they work just as well, until we get our own.

By now, Mr. Gilmer had Sophie saddled and leaned over and cupped his right hand just below the stirrup, I knew what I had to do, trusting my right foot in the firm grip of Mr. Gilmer's right hand, I slid my left foot in the stirrup and slung myself into the saddle. Now, for the first time in my life I was seated atop what I deemed was once a majestic Tennessee Walking Horse, sitting there sorrowful and broken hearted, and with no honor in me. I was glad nobody knew it but me and Mr. Gilmer.

Mr. Gilmer said, "just give her the reins L'l Keesie and let her go, she knows what to do, head her on down to the peanut mill and back." It was about a quarter mile to the peanut mill. To soothe the sorrow of this unfortunate adventure, I apologized to Sophie all the way, and patted her neck incessantly, and begged for forgiveness.

Sophie started off like a tin man on stilts, like a city girl learning to drive a standard shift, starting, lurching, stalling . . . her ancient ankles and knees seemed to be welded together. After about twenty rough paces, I glanced back over her boney haunches at Mr. Gilmer, hoping he would say bring her on back, she ain't ready to ride yet, but Mr. Gilmer pointed sternly toward the peanut mill so we pressed on.

As we made our turn at the peanut mill and started home, Sophie began to kick off a few of the rusty rivets and smooth out the ride a little. I complimented her for fighting through the pain and stiffness the way she did. As I started to pull her over at the barn, Mr. Gilmer pointed stoically to the other end of Reid Street, another quarter mile away. Sophie was still limping a little, her head was still sagging, and her gait was gimpy, but she never complained, so again we pressed on.

We had traveled three fourths a mile when we made the next turn and started home again. It was then that Sophie seemed to shift up into second gear, she magically lifted her head up straight and began to toss it slightly back and forth as if she was beginning to hum a little gospel tune to herself. Her ears perked up and pointed skyward trying to soak up more of the music from above the sky.

She gradually accelerated into a little strut. Man, I thought, look at ol' Sophie stepping out. As we approached the barn, she didn't even glance over, she pranced and paraded right on by Mr. Gilmer, right on back to the peanut mill again.

When we came out of the one mile turn, amazingly, Sophie shifted again. Now she was in third gear and sewing machine smooth. It was a magic carpet ride like I had never experienced, that old red clay was flying up behind her like a moonshiner's hot rod, and her hooves were singing out rhythm like the shoe shine boys at the back street barber shop. Now Sophie was busy sashaying, refining and coordinating her gyrations with her precious memories. She was stretching out more and more, seeking perfection in her gait, becoming more and more familiar with history; her hind legs were beginning to hit the proper stride, dropping her hips, and raising her front end, her front hooves pawing like a puppy treading water. We were cruising along in majestic sovereignty, hovering above ordinary and mundane humanity.

None of her complicated movements affected what was going on in the saddle. You could have set a cold drink on the horn and never spilled a drop. This little puny and pathetic lady had just transformed herself into a majestic Tennessee Walking Horse right before my unbelieving eyes. She was no longer Sophie, she was Sophia.

I began to wish that somebody besides me and Mr. Gilmer could see it. The comfort that I had found in obscurity was now a liability. The presence of the Pelham Journal that I previously abhorred was now a flaming desire. It was truly amazing and remains just that way in my memory.

How quickly our perception of life can change. Sophie was a majestic Tennessee Walking Horse from the very start though I could not see it. It was not my faith that afforded the transformation, it was Mr. Gilmer's. It was not my performance that expressed the reality, it was Sophie's. Many times since that day I have I been the beneficiary of someone else's faith and works, someone whom I have naively or unjustly prejudged. Very slowly, I am learning to eliminate this awful habit of prejudice.

Over the next several weeks Sophie and I became best of friends as I advertised her talents throughout the city. We laughed and talked about old times and dreams for the future. Daily, I combed and curried her smooth and slick and rubbed her down with Mr. Gilmer's special formula of medicated horse liniment.

I led her to vacant lots and obscure patches where the sweet grass grew thick and delicious, and I filled her full of what Mr. Gilmer called sweet feed—ground corn, hay, and molasses. Steadily the sight of her curvy bones disappeared, covered over by thick striations of muscle, as her image grew to meet her inherent majesty.

I treated Sophie to the fundamentals of good health and well—being which lies in a good diet, coupled with exercise, and rest, and a loving and caring companion. Her eyes grew brighter, her head no longer sagged, and her coat glistened in the winter sunshine. She was as happy to see me each day as I was to see her. That's the way it is with friends.

One day in the early spring I came to see her, but she was gone. I suffered through several lonesome days before I found out that Mr. Gilmer sold her to Mr. Fred Hand. He said Mr. Fred witnessed my advertisements up and down Reid Street and made him an offer he could not refuse.

I liked Mr. Fred. I knew him as a man of distinction, a statesman, a prominent business man and civic leader. I saw him often in the Hand Trading Company where I plundered around and played in the elevator and slid down the long spiraling banister until someone hollered for me to move on, and take my dog with me.

But, back then, I knew little of the history that I know now. Thanks in part to Ms. Marion D. Rogers' book, "The Building of a Town", I know some of the history of my hometown. I know now that Mr. Fred (1904-1978) was one of twelve children of Pelham's most famous visionary, Mr. Judson Larrabee Hand (1851-1916). Mr. J.L. Hand arrived in Pelham in 1872, before it was officially named.

Four years before Mr. J.L.'s arrival, Major J. A. Maxwell was surveying for the South Georgia and Florida Railroad Company and came upon a piece of high ground in the dense pine forest between Albany and Thomasville. He recommended to his employer that a flag station be established on that spot and requested permission to name it after Major John Pelham, a friend and fellow soldier who had been killed five years earlier. Major Pelham was JEB Stuart's chief artillery officer. He was killed in action at Kelly's Ford, Virginia at the age of twenty-four. General Robert E. Lee had referred to him as, "the gallant Major Pelham," adding, "It is glorious to see such courage in one so young!"

It is reported that General Stonewall Jackson asked General JEB Stuart, "Have you another Pelham, General? If so I wish you would give him to me! With a Pelham on each flank I believe I could whip the world!"

When Mr. J.L. Hand arrived at the little whistle stop, to be officially named Pelham nine years later, it is likely that he did not suspect that he would be the one to make it famous. It appeared that he had set his mind solely on running a little steam powered saw mill.

To his misfortune his brand new saw mill burned down. He rebuilt it. It burned down again. He rebuilt it again. It burned again. I am not sure how many times it burned, but he continued rebuilding until it quit burning, even when he ran out of money and had to travel to Thomasville to borrow to continue. Apparently, he possessed a plentiful supply of persistence, a supreme necessity if one is to be successful at anything.

Over the next ten years, Mr. J.L. purchased 30,000 acres of land, cutting timber and clearing roughly 3,000 thousand acres for farming. He developed a large turpentine business. He became the largest melon grower in the world, loading thirty box cars daily during the growing season. He became the largest naval stores operator in the south. It seemed that all his investments prospered; cotton gins, fertilizer plants, retail business, railroads, banking, manufacturing, and much more. His freight bill alone for his railroad exports is recorded as $100,000 in 1883.

In 1885, he built a Victorian mansion for his family which could have rivaled any present day historic landmark, but unfortunately it was torn down in 1972. (Thanks to Lee Willis for the picture of the Hand house) Mr. J.L. contributed much to the community by donating land, materials, and money to churches, schools, and charities. Mr. J.L. Hand's final project was a four story 98,300 square foot department store modeled after Chicago's Marshall Field's Store. It became known as the largest rural department store in America.

It fascinated railway travelers to see such a massive structure located in such a small place. It was said, "If you can't find it at Hand Trading Company, then you don't need it." It was completed in January of 1916 and the great visionary passed away ten months later at the age of sixty-five. The Hand Trading Company stands there today as a monument to the entrepreneurial spirit of a great American.

I mention in this writing only a few of Mr. J.L. Hand's many achievements for this is not a book about him, but when a man of his caliber stands up, I am inspired to sit down. I must briefly mention that he became a premier statesman as well, serving in the Georgia State Senate from 1886-1905, in addition to numerous local offices.

His son, Mr. Fred Hand, sat in the same senate chair in 1931 and later in the Georgia House of Representatives from 1947-1955. He was defeated as a gubernatorial candidate for Governor in 1954.

It seemed that Mr. Fred Hand and I shared a singular and fairly insignificant commonality—a love for horses. And to my misfortune, we both fell in love with the same horse.

Sophie's sudden absence was a disappointment that I suspected would come in due time, but I did not think it would come so soon, nor bring with it such distress. I remember it being hard to bear.

When disappointments come they have no compassion, and no concern for convenience. They have but one desire which is to crush us as flat as possible, to empty out all our insides and see what we are really made of. Disappointments cause us to take inventory, to collect the fragments, if we can find them, and to return to the drawing table, and start from scratch again, and try to reconstruct a more resilient constitution.

CHAPTER 7

All my life I have had friends. When I am in need of a friend, one always appears. Neighborhood friends are the most notorious for their appearance. There was my first true friend, Bobby Thomas, the mild mannered and lovable son of Mrs. Joy Thomas, a school teacher who always met me at the door and said, "Bobby has to do his homework, he can't play right now." I never bought into that philosophy; that a man is supposed to work at home.

Home is reserved for the four greatest pleasures in life: eating, laughing, sleeping, and dreaming. Mrs. Joy sat on Bobby like a laying hen and never allowed him to run free and loose like us, like free range bantam roosters. She didn't trust men; not since hers run off and left her with a bunch of young'uns to raise.

Bobby was resourceful and made the best of his incarceration. He nailed a basketball goal on the barn, like prisoners generally do, and he played basketball in the back yard for years and years. Nobody in town could beat him in basketball; pick your game, horse, pig, twenty-one, it don't matter Bobby still wins. Last I heard, Bobby shot seven hundred and forty six free throws without a miss, before he had to go and do his homework.

Bobby's big brother Buddy played football and was rough on Bobby, so Bobby learned to hate football. Bobby said Buddy had a mean streak, like his daddy, and I come to believe it. Buddy loved to thump my ears ever chance he got, but I couldn't hardly blame him for it, everybody did it, they stuck out like stop signs, and the temptation was irresistible for most of mankind.

There was Tommy Humphries, who lived up over the jail. His daddy was fire chief, and his family was awarded that geographic distinction. People in jail always seemed to cuss more and louder than the average man, and I suspect that is where I first got the idea it was not so difficult a craft as people thought. The merry banter that we enjoyed with Pelham's finest citizens substantially enhanced my literary resume.

Tommy wanted to chew tobacco so he could spit like the police downstairs did, but I had already quit by then. I suggested that we mix up some chocolate cocoa and sugar and milk and it would provide us enough spitting material, and nobody would care, as long as we had something to spit. So that's what we did, but it didn't last. The reputation of the police was threatened, they got jealous, and said we were spitting more than the law allowed, and had to quit or be arrested and thrown in with the citizenry. So I quit again, and have since lived in abstinence. I believe a man ought not to chew, if he can help it.

Tommy's memory has managed to recall a treasured toy my daddy brought home from Detroit. I had forgotten, but when he described it, my memory was jolted, and I can see it again.

It was a silver Buick; no, there were two silver Buicks from Detroit, because my little brother Denny had one too. And they were motorized. They even had lights, head lights and tail lights, where you could drive around after everybody else had gone to bed, and still see where you were going.

It was unheard of in Pelham, Georgia in that day for a little boy of my caliber to have a motorized vehicle, with lights. We put over a hundred thousand miles on those Buicks before the lights quit working, then we put another hundred thousand on them in the daylight. The value of high mileage vehicles is a philosophy that has stuck with me.

I do not have space in this little book to remember all my friends; but I still desire to honor them all, one by one, someday, if I can.

I regard my friends as my greatest asset, ninety-five percent of the time. They seem to come from all over, and once they are registered in my book of friendship, they are never erased, ninety-five percent of the time. Wallace Walton is one of the ninety-five per centers'; he entered early and has remained thereafter.

We started first grade together and held each other in high esteem right on through twelve years of hoops; likely, right on up 'til he reads this. It was in fifth grade that Wallace got the notion that we were less than we could be because we did not enjoy the habit of smoking. Smoking was old hat to many of those who modeled manhood for us. They constantly reported its benefits to us and hammered us for our unmanliness. We remained skeptics, clung to our guns and religious superstitions, and stiff armed their relentless solicitations for a length of time worthy of merit, but none came. Now, seeing no merit in our abstinence, we decided to go ahead and see for ourselves if there was anything to it.

We searched deep in the bowels of the couch and all our dresser drawers for pennies, sold a few drink bottles, pooled our resources and scrounged up twenty six cents, the price of a pack of Camels at the Consolidated Drug Store. I was the designated buyer because I bought cigarettes all the time for various relatives. No one would ever suspect I was buying them to smoke.

Wallace did not fit the profile, he would be suspect, and to further the risk, his father worked just a couple doors down at Giggy's clothing store;and his mother just across the street at the dime store. Wallace waited safely out of sight at Mr. Story's Western Auto store.

I should have known better than to test a promising new adventure with Wallace, but I was an optimist then. I remember a time when my cousins and I threw a rope over a large chinaberry limb about twenty feet up, and cultivated the delightful habit of swinging off the roof of the barn for months, until Wallace came and tried it; and it broke, and promptly ended the adventure.

I remember my neighbors and friends popping thousands of firecrackers year after year, until Wallace came and popped one in his hand, and shut down that enterprise as well; we could play baseball in the back yard, days on end without incident, until Wallace appeared and a line drive to the face was as common as spit.

Once, in Cub Scouts, Wallace was in charge of a project. It was a traditional low risk Cub Scout activity; and for anybody else, it would have proceeded without a hitch.

Wallace went to the saw mill and brought back a sawed off log so we could count the rings and determine the age of the tree. The log was about the size and dimension of one of mama's chocolate cakes but weighed a good deal more. After we counted the rings and estimated the specimen to be about twenty years old, we assumed the novelty had expired.

But Wallace's mind was always more alive with possibilities. He announced that the log was not used up yet, and enumerated a series of speculations concerning its future. He calculated that the next best option was to roll it off the top of the club house and see how far it would roll.

It began as an innocent adventure, as did all of Wallace's ideas, but disaster lurked close by as always, awaiting the green light from Wallace. As the specimen gained momentum and bounded off the roof, Stanley showed up just in time to absorb the momentum just above his left eye. I was certain by the blood trail that Dr. Brim would need his needle and thread. The wounded Cub Scout managed to stagger the forty yards home where his mother answered his wails, performed first aid, and attempted to calm his frazzled spirit.

We were commanded to march to Stanley's house and repent for our misadventure and seek forgiveness. There, we saw his petite mother rocking him gently in her lap and singing softly to him, while pressing a damp cloth against his bulging forehead. Not one of us could think of the proper words of repentance, so we shyly formed a sympathetic Cub Scout semi—circle, and watched and waited on each other to step forward with the apology.

Stanley was a stout young cub, and as time marched slowly around our semi—circle, I studied the details of this sad scenario. Soon, I was gripped with a strange sense of amusement at the contrast between him and his mother, her small bundle of dense and delightful compassion being swallowed up by his grieving and whimpering bulk. It looked like a bushel of corn had been poured into a half bushel basket.

Stanley's sweet, heartbroken mother continued singing the little lullaby, gently rocking her only son, barely acknowledging our presence. We remained frozen, persecuted by the unending silence, none of us brave enough to break it. We were held hostage for what seemed like an eternity. After this long and uneasy spell of justice, Stanley's mother slowly raised her eyes from the one she loved and began to carefully study our faces.

One by one she examined our countenance to see if she could discover the culprit and determine if he was due justice or mercy. There was no change in her expression until she came to Wallace. When she saw that Wallace was in attendance, she was overcome with pity, and despaired for the rest of us, who she deemed innocent, or at the worst, guilty by association. She reluctantly announced that she held no malice for the lot of us, and pardoned us, admonishing us with the impossible task of trying to be more careful next time. We all broke and ran before she changed her mind.

In due time, it became quite evident to me that most of the time I spent with Wallace, I was asking for forgiveness for something; nevertheless, he was never deterred or discouraged by the incessant phenomenon that followed him wherever he went;

and his busy mind persisted in dreaming up one fascinating possibility after another.

As prospective smokers now packing a brand new pack of Camels, we began our search for a secure place to launch our virgin cruise. My optimism teamed up with my wisdom as I suggested that we smoke our historic cigarette in the loneliest place in town; a place where everybody avoided at every opportunity—under Daddy Powell's house at the central cleanout valve— a domain where I remained the sole visitor. It was an ingenious perspective, except for one defect of which I was unaware. A sizable knot had recently popped out of the old heart pine flooring under Daddy Powell's bedroom and he had not had time to plug it.

Cloaked in imaginary security, we lit up and puffed steadily on that handsome Camel, searching in vain for the advertised pleasure. The celestial joy that our friends so boldly prophesied eluded us somehow. Not to be so easily defeated, we lit up again, this time with two Camels a piece, one in each side of our mouth. We anticipated a double dose of pleasure which mysteriously never materialized.

After smoking three cigarettes in succession, I considered myself qualified to make an informed decision. I surmised then and more so now that smoking is about the dumbest thing a man can do; that no semi-conscious creature would ever smoke more than three cigarettes, and any reasonably intelligent creature would bail out after one. I made myself a note then and there to never take advice from a smoker.

It is good policy and has served me well. When a smoker gives me advice there is a little neon footnote that flashes in my mind saying, "what the hell does he know, he's a smoker . . . I don't care if he is the President."

I was about to express my disappointment and promptly end my smoking career, when I heard a door slam and saw legs walking around the house and approaching the entrance to our hide out.

There was immediately a sense of awareness in the owner of the legs by the familiarity of the gait; the awareness extended to cover the intended direction, and the ensuing results.

We knew we were had, as they say in some circles; and we knew we were in need on an attorney, but we had no money for one. We had unwisely invested it all in Camel stock. And this was long before the government fell in love with transgressors, and took to pursuing petty cases, and charging the tax payers for its' liberal benevolence and reckless extravagance.

As you have suspected the legs belonged to Daddy Powell. At first, he thought the house was on fire, but upon further notice he suspected the ensuing conspiracy. He put his ear to the knot hole, heard us coughing and mumbling between our coughs and wisely deciphered our plot.

"Boys", he said, "ya'll come on out before you burn the house down, and bring them Camels, I'm 'bout outta smokes." These are some of the hallowed words that cancelled my career as a smoker. There were some additional words of rebuke spoken eloquently by Daddy Powell, but my recent Christian training prohibits me from repeating them.

Since he inherited a new pack of camels out of the deal, he saw no need to publish our delinquency to the rest of the world, like I have just done here. But it is of no consequence, for now, Wallace and I have a resume of much greater sins that remains unpublished.

The credit for my tobacco free status must be awarded to the one most responsible. It was Wallace to whom I give the credit. He succeeded in beginning and ending my smoking career all in the same day.

Today, I remain free from the slavery of tobacco, but I can take no credit. God bless Wallace; and you too, if you have helped to save a man from the slavery of addiction.

By the time I reached fifth grade, all of my dark and devious notions had migrated underground, lavishly residing in spacious private housing, out of public view, well trained to evade and deceive authority. Consequently, Mrs. Bostick, my fifth grade teacher, regarded me as a model student, a near angel as far as she could tell. I enjoyed this persona for nearly three-fourths of the school year, until that spring when everything thawed out and came to life, including my covert devilishment.

On that fateful Friday, in the boy's bathroom, three of us were apprehended by the principal, Mr. D.D. Morrison. Mr. Morrison roamed the halls of Pelham Elementary School in those days like a roaring lion seeing who he could devour. It was rumored that the initials in his name stood for "Dead Dog", which is what you became if he ever caught you in error.

I was somewhat personally acquainted with Mr. Morrison. During our last appointment, which was distant but memorable, we had reminisced my resume as it related to citizenship. At that meeting, I remembered him issuing mild compliments, as he noted that lately my office visits had grown fewer and further between. He appeared surprised but delighted and smiled between each sentence.

It was a part of his nature to smile between each sentence and had no particular bearing on his sentiments or his intentions, anybody who visited his office could tell that. He could smile just as well as he whipped you as he could when complimented you.

Returning to the bathroom adventure, I well recall not only that infamous day, but the days that led up to it. The infraction occurred in the boy's bathroom nearest the cafeteria just after lunch. The adventure began spontaneously on a Monday, and was such a hit, that it was repeated for five days running.

It would have occurred to thoughtful young men that the laws of probability have no respect for persons. We should have known that our luck would run out, but we were all optimists back then, optimists of the worst kind, stubbornly naïve optimists. The general temptation which plagues the optimist of this sort is to discount or ignore the facts, and to advertise his sunny disposition an expression of faith.

Mr. Morrison caught us red handed, or I should say wet handed. We were lined up shoulder to shoulder, me, Sonny, and Ladon, musketeers we were, the three of us, our backs to the entrance, three paces from a window which was four feet from the floor. We were collectively focused on our endeavor, engaged in a heated competition, seeing who could be first to pee out the window.

A crowd had gathered to cheer us on as the battle was strenuous and we were in need of regular inspiration. A guard was posted at the entrance to whistle and alert us should the authorities approach, but the boisterous cloud of witnesses unintentionally muffled his alarm. It was such great fun that no one noticed Mr. Morrison's attendance, except the watchman who conveniently remembered that he had business elsewhere, tipped his hat upon Mr. Morrison's entry, and politely excused himself.

I am not sure how long Mr. Morrison enjoyed the competition, but he was reverent enough to let us pee ourselves out as he quietly dismissed each cheerleader, tapping them on the shoulder one by one and giving them the thumb. Now it was just the four of us. The silence alerted us to the fact that we were in deep need of an advocate. Advocates were rare in those days, and expensive, and the current expenditure was not budgeted. Optimists often operate in a deficit.

We saw no alternative except to plead guilty and fall on the mercy of the court which for me personally was the habitual mode of operation. There were no families in our community named Miranda in those days, nor did we possess the faintest knowledge that the powers of litigation could concoct a successful defense by simply blaming our transgressions on someone else, or on some rare, random genome.

What Mr. Morrison did not know at the time was that the peeing contest had begun on Monday and advanced merrily through the week. Now it was Friday. He had missed the regular season. What he so luckily wandered into was the final quarter of the playoffs, or should I say, peeoffs. Had he tarried another two minutes he would have missed the entire spectacle, and we would have gone free. Life sometimes boils down to small fractions of time.

It is natural for young men to be competitive. It is natural for young bladders to be the fullest and most competitive just after lunch. It is natural then to be curious as to who can stand the furthest from the toilet and still hit the mark. That is how the contest began.

At first, the competition was one dimensional, for distance alone. Contestants fired from one step back, then two, then, three and etc. I think Ladon took the prize in the preliminaries at about six paces. His bladder was exceptional, a marvel to envy.

As creativity kicked in, we began incorporating a more comprehensive realm of dimensions, namely, height, accuracy, endurance, no hands, writing your name on the wall, filling someone's lunch box, and on and on through the gamut of a fifth grade mind.

At the time of our arrest, we were attempting to arch it out a four foot window from three feet away. It is a joy now to remember how much pressure a young bladder can naturally produce and sustain. There was always pressure to spare as I recall. Back then, we never suspected that one day we would lose it, and have the insatiable longing we have now to repossess it, and watch with envious pleasure as we instruct our grandsons how to pee discretely against the back side of a tree.

Mr. Morrison invited us to attend a revival in his office, and we responded admirably. We mutually agreed that revival was just the very thing that we desired at the time. No revival can be successful unless a fair amount of prayer precedes it. We began to supply it fervently.

Upon the fifth period bell, as our redeemed friends engaged in the study of geography, Mr. Morrison began the service promptly, as would any good evangelist, reminding us that there is such a thing as righteousness, and that we had ventured far from it.

Again, we mutually agreed and affirmed that his theology was impeccable. All the while we were incredibility lonesome for geography. We began to miss it terribly and longed to reunite with it more so now than we ever thought we would.

Mr. Morrison was not content to pay a quick and casual front porch visit and dismiss our iniquities as we so ardently preferred, no sir, he opened the front door, entered the house, and rambled about throughout the place, going from room to room, violating our privacy, magnifying our deficiencies far beyond that of common and average sin. According to his diagnosis, we had progressed now into a realm of degradation that put us on the brink of purgatory.

It was his conviction that we had underestimated the depth and breadth of our sinfulness. We had not accurately measured the distance from east to west. We thought that we had barely traveled out of the city limits with our little bag of sins. To our surprise, he detected us approaching Istanbul with a box car full.

He surmised that we were much greater sinners now than when he first laid eyes on us, and that we were traveling down the wrong road at the speed of light. He saw it as his appointed duty to throw out the anchor here and now or else we would be in Shaing Hi by nightfall and lost forever. We tried to appear appreciative that he was so noble and so loyal to his duty.

Eventually, the fire in his words sufficiently scorched the entire congregation. Following this lengthy tirade which extends beyond my ability to recite it now, Mr. Morrison felt better, having relieved himself of the load that was on his mind.

He slowly began to cool, and to unbuckle his belt. Once he had awakened it from its customary civilian duty, and our eyes from their random orbit, he snatched it violently through its maneuvers, making those dreaded rhythmic sounds as it exited each loop. He doubled it, held it directly before us by the doubled ends, and demonstrated his ability to make audacious popping sounds which quickly provoked memories of a most painful sort, the kind of memories you would like to forget, if you could.

We would have promptly peed on ourselves if we could, but thankfully we were all peed out at the moment. By now, all hope was gone. I resigned myself to the fact that after this lashing I was about to receive I would make my bed in reform school for the remainder of the year.

I began to be more thoughtful and to think outside myself, where I should have thought previously, where life objectively exists. I thought of my wonderful teacher, Mrs. Bostick, who was considering me for superlatives, what disappointment she would now suffer, and I thought of my humble mother who would hardly ever be able to raise her head again in public because of her son's transgressions. I thought of my brethren on either side, suffering likewise. I thought of the impoverished little children of China who would have more graciously respected and honored the indoor plumbing that I so blatantly and repeatedly desecrated.

Eventually, my thoughts arrived at a most familiar place, the place where I always arrive, the place where I always wonder . . . how is it that I can do good for days, and weeks, and even months, and then one day carelessly step outside my righteous consistency and into that dark corridor that seems to run parallel to every good deed; you know the dark corridor of which I speak, the one happily disguised as a new and novel adventure.

How could I have not recognized it for what it was? Certainly there was something that lived within me that delighted in pushing me into places that I did not want to go, but I could not seem to resist.

As I pondered this conundrum, hopelessly mired deep in helplessness, a wondrous supernatural event occurred. Mr.

Morrison grew still and silent and sighed mournfully, as he appeared to meditate upon the vastness of our sad and sorry deficiencies. He sat at length upon the front of his desk before us, puzzled.

His eyes became moist and glistened as the large clock on the wall behind him ran off with the rest of fifth period. I glanced timidly and apologetically into his eyes and caught a glimpse of my own reflection. His eyes seemed to grow more and more content and satisfied with the mystery that was transforming his mind. I did not understand then, nor do I now, how the rational eyes of justice merge fluently, and seamlessly, and harmoniously with the restorative eyes of mercy.

I knew the understanding eyes of mercy; I had seen them in my mother. I knew the piercing eyes of justice; I had seen them in my father. But never before this day had I witnessed both sets of eyes homogenized like this in the same person. This was new.

I began to entertain a strange notion. I thought, perhaps Mr. Morrison saw his reflection in our eyes, or more practically, he saw himself in us. Perhaps Mr. Morrison had found himself, at some previously appointed time, precisely in the same predicament that we were in just now, just a heartbeat from hell. Perhaps he remembered that somebody graciously offered him something that was beyond his ability to produce, perhaps at some historic, predestined time someone offered him the only way out, the hand of Grace . . . marvelous . . . wonderful . . . amazing Grace.

There was something going on in that little room that I could not explain. Mr. Morrison was not the only authority in attendance. There was a third party there that day, one with more authority and more power than Mr. Morrison. This new party bound us together, saint and sinner alike, and united us as kindred souls. This same Visitor joins us just now, as I write, and as you read, reminding us that it is far better for us all to be one heart beat from Heaven, than one heart beat from hell.

We reaped the most appropriate harvest from our sowing as Mr. Morrison assigned us to staying after school and cleaning the bath room. I cannot recall the length of the sentence, but it was sufficient. I thought that the revival service was sufficient in itself, but Mr. Morrison needed a little more insurance.

During my new after school duty, I began to prepare my defense for the higher court and a more formidable prosecutor. I would now have to face my mother. She was nearly omniscient. She could hardly ever be deceived. I would have to be clever and crafty.

Mama always relied on the old tried and true proverbs. In cases like this, it was, "give a man enough rope and he will hang himself." I knew also that I must proceed quickly for news of this variety has the ability to outrun ordinary news and get home before me.

Providence again guarded over me and secured the moment and left it in my hands to construct the proper narrative. By the time I arrived home I had prepared the appropriate short story. The plan was to confess partially, but not entirely, and to transfer the blame, like the politicians teach. Subtlety, and modesty, and brevity were of the essence as I gave mamma the short and sanitized version.

I casually shrugged it all off as just another day at school, that Mr. Morrison just happened to come by and talk with some of us about lingering in the rest room a little too long after lunch.

Parents prefer to give their children the benefit of the doubt when they can.

Until such a time as they realize a child will say anything to save his butt. It was mama's policy to listen far more often than she spoke, to listen intently with her honest eyes searching the blank spaces between your words, and examining the darting of your eyes, the inconsistencies of your mannerisms, changes in your respiration and heart rate, like a human lie detector.

Mama listened insightfully to my short story until I was able to convince her that I was guilty of something, though she was not yet sure what it was. I was always impressed with my mother's patience as she was content to wait, knowing the truth will soon rise to the surface.

She finally addressed the issue briefly in her classical style saying, "Son, if Sonny jumps in the fire, will you jump in to?" Apparently something in my confession led her to believe that Sonny had hatched the idea. I cannot remember what it was. Sins of omission are the easiest to forget.

Of course, the answer to the proverbial "jumping into the fire" is a resounding "no" in the plush comfort of theoretical speculation, but not so resolute in the harsh confines of concrete reality. To this very day, none of my friends have ever jumped into a fire in my presence, thereby relieving me of the necessity of that decision.

They have, however, tested the spirit of the question by jumping naked into the forbidden waters of the American Legion swimming pool at midnight when the gates were locked and criminal trespass was the only way in. Such immoral and illegal adventures are the perpetual specialty of friends and the seductive power of their creative concoctions is difficult to resist.

I have found myself on various occasions thumping about in a ripe watermelon patch at midnight searching for the plumpest specimen to borrow from a generous donor, but, now I have digressed severely. Nevertheless, I escaped the rest room caper with my life intact, and it slipped into history filed away with an unending, unmentionable compendium of sins, all filed away in a thick folder under the heading of Grace.

The Hand Trading Company

The Hand House

Mom Powell and Daddy Powell

David, Cheryl, Dennis, Philip, Terry, Spencer

Red Marshall, Dennis, Scout

Cheryl, Scout

CHAPTER 8

At the mature age of twelve I found myself in the newspaper business. It was a monumental day because I have never had an ambition or an inclination for business. It was monumental in a second way, a more profound way—it was from that day forward that I was unable to shake myself free from the curse of permanent employment, accurately confirming the biblical prophecy that a man will earn his bread by the sweat of his brow.

I can say without reservation that I did not purposefully pursue the newspaper business, not by any initiative of my own. It pursued me. Providence is that way, He will not let you rest; He will corner you, and hound you, and press you into some direction that you did not plan to go. And punish you if you resist.

And one cannot ignore the magnetic power of friendship. Friends desire accomplices, they suck you into whatever it is that they have been sucked into as the previous chapter demonstrated.

But, occasionally, it is a good thing, particularly when friends serve as the agents of Providence.

At the mature age of twelve I saw no great necessity in squandering my fleeting youth with working, when playing had proven itself so great a profit. But, as it often is, I was sucked into the newspaper business by a friend, Jimmy Warren.

Jimmy lived conveniently, just thirty steps beyond my back door, and was just the kind of friend who always desired a smile to match his. He could not seem to live without a smile on his face, nor the absence of one on yours. Jimmy was one of the few friends my age who was smaller than I was.

Jimmy lived in a little concrete block house with his mother, two little sisters, and a little brother. I never met his father, Jimmy said he had run off and never came back, leaving the family to do the best they could. I never could understand how a man could run off and leave his family exposed to the evils of the world. It is a thought that haunts me from time to time. If I could correct it, I would not be writing this book, but that one.

I was unaware at the time that Jimmy's newspaper money was often a basic part of their grocery budget. The baby at the time, little Suzie, never learned to walk or talk, but she wore the same eternal smile that the rest of the family wore, which left no doubt that she had blended happily into this loving family. I remember asking mama, " how come little Suzie is so happy when she cannot walk or talk and has no daddy." Mama said, "all little Suzie knows is the people she loves, love her enough." I reckon there ain't no finer answer than that. True love never fails.

I entered the newspaper business where I normally enter things, at the lowest rung on the ladder. It was the Grit paper. I know that the modern world is unfamiliar with the Grit paper. Those who knew it then were generally unimpressed with it, and would barely give more than a grunt or shrug if they could remember it now.

I can barely remember it myself, even when I try. It is not a great memory for it was not a great paper. The idea did eventually come into its own. But back then, it was a thin and faint facsimile of the current USA Today paper, exceptionally thin and faint as I recall.

I did not know enough to know that I was peddling an unpopular publication and was blatantly unashamed. I proceeded to promote and circulate that poor publication with such vigor that I stirred up the imaginations of the local publishers. They began to offer me better wages to peddle their papers.

I was attentive to their offers and filled with pride to have market value. I began to study my Cub Scout book of virtues, and determined that loyalty was reserved for personal relationships, and did not apply to free market ventures; just how I determined that I cannot remember, but it is likely related to my well-developed talent for rationalization.

The next winner of the prize of my employment was the Thomasville Times/Enterprise, a daily evening paper, except for Sunday. On Sunday, it pushed me out of bed at a most miserable hour, an hour reserved only for hunting squirrels, and for long prayers of repentance for the things I said about the newspaper business.

At first, the papers arrived shortly after school just a half mile from my house at the bus station on the corner of Matheson Avenue and the old famous Dixie Highway, the umbilical cord to anything north and south. After a short while, for some unknown reason, the conspirators transferred a mile and a half north to Ed Langley's service station on the north side of town.

The papers were delivered to us by a lean stranger with lock jaw and a hefty contempt for juveniles. He arrived in a white panel truck and left the motor running as he tossed out several bailed packets of papers. The several bails always landed face up with the last name of each courier printed in bold print. It was the only thing ever personal to me about the newspaper business. A man always enjoys seeing his name in bold print.

Somewhere about midway through my tenure as a newspaper man I took a promotion to the Albany Herald. The prestige was a tad better, but the work and pay was about the same, a fairly routine occurrence for most of my promotions thereafter.

A paper boy has four assets besides an average or below mentality—a fast and dependable bicycle, a good throwing arm, a rain coat, and a superior guard dog. I had a superior guard dog. I mentioned him in my first book. He had no patience with dogs that attempted to disrupt our deliveries. He routinely chewed on their ear until their patience improved. I thoroughly enjoyed those counseling sessions. My memory records them as the highlights of that era.

I don't know exactly when it was that I retired from the newspaper business, but I do remember the circumstances. I do remember that I gave myself over to it for nearly two years, a time sufficient enough to develop affection for it. But I never did.

The newspaper business was memorable enough that I have not since had any desire to reunite with it. You may recall that two years to a juvenile is an exceedingly long time, and could not slip by as easily then, as it can now.

Perhaps my most memorable day in the newspaper business was the day that I decided to retire. It was one of those days so memorable that all the details are illuminated in technicolor.

It was cold and wet and more miserable than any day ever should be. I was cold, and wet, and tired, and hungry, and lonesome for chicken noodle soup. I was in a hurry to get at it. I went straight to work after school inadvertently giving my bodyguard the day off.

Ol' Butch, the brindle mongrel, had challenged Speck only once before and had half an ear to show for it; thereafter he cowered under the front porch dreaming of the day that Speck would have an appointment elsewhere, and he could express his revenge to me personally.

On this day, seeing me unguarded, he rejoiced, and revived from his depression, and lit out after me to release all that pent up rage. My old Western Flyer was as cold and tired as I was, and could not rise up to meet this challenge. It tried, I will give it credit for that, but it just could not do it; the sprocket was too far gone and the chain did not respond well to stress; particularly the level of stress that fell upon it so suddenly.

In just a short while, the chain jumped off its old worn out track and left me floating downstream without a paddle. Ol' Butch took advantage of my helplessness and grabbed hold of the cuff of my britches and commenced to gnawing and growling and shaking. I commenced beating him across the face with all I had, the Albany Herald. He was not impressed with the Herald. I do not think he would have been impressed with the Grit either, or even the New York Times. A newspaper which cannot impress a dog has reached its lowest ebb. Because of the waning value of newspapers I began to entertain thoughts of retirement. Others should consider it.

Butch jerked my britches leg every which way until my feet slipped off the pedals. Every little boy dreads the occasion when his feet slip off the pedals. All the weight is then transferred to the crossbar. The body parts which are required to absorb the force are not designed for that purpose and are quick to squeal and complain.

I think it was the intensity and consistency of my shrieks that alerted Mr. Edwards who finally pulled the mongrel off me. Here was the very moment that I began to formulate my retirement from the newspaper business.

My tenure as a newspaper man, however, was a good thing for I learned sooner rather than later the fundamentals of enterprise. I learned about investment and return. I learned to balance a budget. I did not think at the time that it was a complicated idea; I thought that it was a practical reality. But what did I know, I was just a twelve year old kid, how could I have known what politicians know—just blame the other party for the unbalanced budget and pass the whole mess on to the next generation.

Above all, the newspaper business taught me how much sweat was in each dollar I earned. I have surmised as well that this piece of relevant information has not crossed the minds of our present governing officials.

After the newspaper business, without a vacation, and without any market research, I went into the theatre business. It was the natural thing to do. My mother worked at the Park Theatre selling tickets when the regular ticket seller was sick or playing hooky.

My Uncle Winston and Aunt Mildred managed the theaters for a one-eared, cigar-eating entrepreneur from Thomasville. I called him Mr. Gnat because he was small and buzzed around in a kind of worrisome way, sometimes. But, Mr. Nat was a fascinating man and entertained me with adventurous short stories. He had a dozen or more theaters and named them all four letter words. He knew a lot of four letter words. I went on to meet a great many theater patrons who were also fond of four letter words.

Uncle Winston ran the Park Theatre across from the train depot and the Pike Drive-in at the northern city limits. I was contracted to work both locations as needed. The Pike was the infamous drive-in where people went to play bingo and then disappear from view. I knew they were there somewhere, I just could not see them with the windows fogged up.

Occasionally, they would work up an appetite and stop fogging long enough to load up on popcorn and soda, but soon they would dive back into their cubby hole and go to fogging again.

Eventually, this lover's paradise fell under the judgment of God and was hit by a tornado. Newspapers came from all around to take pictures. The marquee read, NOW PLAYING "GONE WITH THE WIND". Like the city of Sodom, they never rebuilt it.

I was vaguely familiar with the theater business prior to becoming employed there. I had stumbled around in the theater workers' way when mama sold tickets. I determined that the supreme benefit for a theater worker was all the popcorn and Coca Cola his belly could hold. Upon my regular employment, I became the most indulgent welfare recipient. You are likely aware of the addictive nature of picture show popcorn. Like any addiction, it quickly multiplies and intensifies with availability. Legalize an addiction and see if things get better.

Uncle Winston carried a pistol in one hip pocket and a half pint of whiskey in the other. I never saw him use the pistol. I cannot say the same for the whiskey. Apparently, managing a picture show and the fury of four females required quite a bit of whiskey.

He really never needed the pistol when Aunt Mildred was around. She was more powerful than a pistol; she was a double barreled shotgun. If you got out of line in the picture show she would let you have both barrels. Aunt Mildred could put a man in his proper place more effectively and more efficiently than anybody I knew. She could speak any language you preferred to speak and speak it fluently, and boldly, and abundantly. She was a sharpshooter whose words went straight to the bull's eye. She never missed her target.

Everyone who confronted her walked away defeated and dismayed; their wits in shreds; holding their butt with both hands; puzzled over their inability to hold their own with such a rare, feisty woman.

When she was not chewing on unruly patrons, she was filling the airwaves with laughter. Her humor was shocking and penetrating. You carried it around with you forever. She was unforgettable, a one of a kind, an ace in the hole. She always come through in a pinch and never failed to bail you out of the blues.

She was so notoriously frank that she often ruffled the feathers of some boisterous movie goers. Consequently, some people did not like her. Aunt Mildred taught me many great lessons that I remember today, one in particular. "Terry", she told me one day, "there are some people that you just don't want as friends. We all need enemies, they keep us motivated!" I came to believe that she truly relished the fact that certain people did not like her. But to those of us who knew her best, she was the most lovable character you could ever hope to meet.

Mildred had three daughters who insured a constancy of household conversations and modulated them several decibels above ours. Mama had a rule that we take the noise outside. I surmised that there was no noise policy in the Willis household. When it got to a fever pitch, Grandmother Huey would calmly remark, "now let's not tell Ruby about it!" Of course, Ruby lived next door and was already familiar with the absence of policy.

The oldest sibling, Lydia was about a year younger than I was, and Dale and Cathy came along fairly quickly thereafter, making the three standing side by side appear to be standing on door steps. Little Winston came along a while later as if he was unexpected and out of place. But he took advantage of his uniqueness and seized the day and milked it dry.

When suitors came to court the girls, little Winston specialized in making himself a nuisance until he was bought off. He was clever and resourceful. He would promise to disappear for a nickel which would buy him a popsicle at Ed Langley's service station. He worked this routine successfully for years and profited greatly. He earned the nickname "Bean" who apparently was a similarly resourceful cartoon character of that day.

When Grandmother Huey moved in with Aunt Mildred, Lydia laid first claim on her, and fenced her off as private property, not allowing the rest of the family equal access. Everybody knew it, but Lydia and Grandmother Huey could never see the thing as a matter of objectivity. They preferred to judge the inequity from their lighthouse of subjectivity.

We cannot cast stones for we all have our favorites and are guilty in some degree. Lydia never went lacking for representation. Grandmother Huey always covered for her. When cookies were baked, Grandmother Huey held a supply in escrow for Lydia.

On one rare occasion sweet muffins were baked and quickly consumed before Lydia's arrival and before Grandmother Huey could squirrel away a few for later. I suspect that it was a grand conspiracy concocted by a couple of second fiddlers.

When Lydia smelled the evidence of sweet muffins and went to retrieve hers, she found the cupboard bare and marched about the place ranting and raving. Lydia was intimately familiar with the proverb, "the squeaky wheel gets the grease!"

On this occasion she desired more grease than abided indoors, so she opened the side door to let Ruby in on it, and began to bellow, "Dale and Cathy ate my sweet . . ." but she never got the word "muffin" out of her mouth for her mouth was quickly filled with the back side of Aunt Mildred's judicious hand. This is a fair representation of how Aunt Mildred operated. There is no exaggeration to it. Many witnesses will confirm it.

During my several years in the theatre business, I enjoyed an array of benefits uncommon in the natural world of employment, particularly for one so juvenile.

I had a ring side seat to every movie that came down the Pike, at least before it was sucked up suspiciously by the tornado. But the Park was much more durable, and lived on, and afforded me educational opportunities that were unparalleled in that day. Fortunately for me and my generation, movies of that day were generally inspirational, and drove home the very same values my parents bought into.

Movies expanded my vocabulary and memory and various cognitive skills more sufficiently than the rigors of school work. Though I could not remember my schoolwork from yesterday, I could quote lines and describe scenes from movies from last year. The incentive of popularity explains the difference. I discovered that I could draw quick and cheap attention from my friends and relatives that way. In a short while, I became a precocious little twerp, like the stars themselves often do, when they become addicted to the elitism of socially accepted hypocrisy.

Movies today are of a different breed. They are mostly ill bred mutants. Movies goers today are being cheated, and robbed, and stripped of their chance to grow character. Movies today blatantly market and promote pretense as a valuable commodity. Yet they are remarkably successful in convincing our children and grandchildren that a man need not be something in reality, but put up a puffy façade and stand behind it and watch the world go ape over it.

I knew well all the heroes of the big screen in my day. The usual ones: Roy and Dale, Gene, Lash Larue, Lone Ranger and Tonto, Zorro, Tarzan, (don't forget Jane) and of course, the three stooges; and on and on into infinity.

But the supreme hero to me was Audie Murphy. He stands alone at the apex of heroism. It is because he was more than an actor. His heroics were real. Before his career in the movies, he was the most decorated combat soldier in World War II.

In the winter of 1945, in southeast France, Murphy's company was attacked by six German tanks and waves of infantry. Lt. Murphy ordered his men to withdraw and find cover, but he remained, and continued the fight.

Commanderring a burning tank, he manned its .50 caliber machine gun and killed or wounded approximately fifty of the enemy. Wounded himself, he retrieved his company, reorganized them, and led them in a counter attack forcing the enemy to retreat.

Audie Murphy was one of nine children born to a Texas sharecropper in the midst of the depression. He had to quit school to work and help support his family. He entered the military as a common foot soldier and left it three years later, wounded three times , but decorated with every honor the military had to offer—thirty-three in all. But that's not all, even foreign countries such as France and Belgium recognized his valor and gave him awards.

It is very easy to make a hero out of a man like Murphy. If you have never heard of him, you should google him and learn more.

The theatre business turned my face into a common and popular commodity. Like the postman, everybody knew me. I learned only a portion of the names of the people who knew mine. I became the boy next door to everybody within a twenty mile radius. I developed more friendships during that short span of time than any one man could ever maintain.

I began to notice particularly the coveys of little chickadees that paraded in and out of the place. I saw fit to invest a little research time in the art of flirtation and became fairly proficient at it. Soon I had one lassoed.

Suzanne was my first true love, she captured my heart and the rest of me just stumbled along behind it. I was certain it would last a lifetime. Suzanne was the sheriff's daughter and had recently moved just down the street from my house. She was a country girl from the small city of Hinsonton, Ga., very near the larger metropolis of Cotton. Suzanne could handle a horse better than any of us city cowboys. She loved her horse unconditionally, the way a man loves his bird dog. She rode circles around us, always giggling and teasing and taunting.

Suzanne radiated adventure, her eyes daring you to race her, her smile making it worth the challenge. She was rough and rugged externally but gentle and kind in nature, the perfect paradox, the very paradox that always woos me.

She usually wore her hair pulled back tight in a ponytail, but when she opened the gate in the evening and turned it out to pasture those long thick strands blossomed out in all directions and ran like honey down her sun tanned shoulders. I thought that she was the prettiest girl I had ever seen and would ever see.

We walked to and from school morning, noon, and afternnoon. She laughed constantly at all my silly stories, convincing me that she liked me, though maybe not as much as I liked her. I became goofy with happiness. It was an alien sensation which I desired to perpetuate.

But as fate would have it, Providence quickly intervened and severed the union leaving me dismayed, puzzled and paralyzed. I could never figure how her neighbor Jack was able to wrestle her from me with so little effort. I knew that she had a lingering affection for Revis, but where did this phantom Jack come from. I could never explain it. I am content now that Providence dropped the hammer on it. He always has the better eye and the upper hand.

Suzanne and Jack have been happily married now for nearly half a century, ever since she came back from Viet Nam. That Viet Nam part is simply foolishness, don't believe it, I just put it there to see if Suzanne would laugh at one of my silly stories one more time.

It wasn't long before I found myself in love with another woman; it's hard for most men to live without one, nearly as hard as living with one. Again, I was like a blind man groping around in the darkness, a drunk on a roller coaster. I grappled my way through each day dumfounded, and wandered about aimlessly trying to keep my mind off her, trying to find an effective remedy so that I could function at some level of proficiency.

I never did find a remedy for it and don't know yet if there is one. I believe it is a road we must travel alone and stumble along until we come out of the fog and see clearly again.

This mesmerizing female was at least ten years my elder, maybe fifteen, but that is of little concern to a man in love. She was way out of my league, but the challenge seemed to stimulate me. She showed up unexpectedly one day at Mr. David Chambliss's service station across the street from my house. She homesteaded there twenty-eight days as the radiant Miss February, boldly displaying her credentials on the Ridgid Tool Company calendar hanging just to the left of the drink machine.

She had a brand new pipe wrench in her hand and seductively straddled a box full of tools at her feet. She smiled broadly and beautifully and I smiled likewise whenever our eyes met, though my eyes were often busy elsewhere. You could tell that she was proud to be a representative of the Ridgid Tool Company.

She had only one problem that I observed, the universal problem that all attractive women face. She had a wagon load of admirers. I was not the only one in love with her; saints and sinners alike lined up like tax payers on April 15. Every man who entered the station went directly to her and admired her tools, even deacons, especially deacons. They spoke admirably of the pipe wrench she held in her hand. They inquired of her availability for plumbing their private facilities.

There was considerable discussion concerning her wardrobe; specifically whether it would stand up and perform its present service under the rigors of heavy construction. The consensus was that it was doubtful. So skimpy was her attire that a cold front would have frozen her stiff.

I could never determine how my fellow admirers could focus on the attributes of her pipe wrench or her pair of pliers when her personal attributes were so outstanding. She was the kind of woman that made a man more grateful for good eyesight.

Certainly, she was improperly attired for plumbing; being a plumber myself I knew that much. But she was properly and skillfully attired to make a man stop for a minute or two and wonder if he needed a new monkey wrench. This is the bait, the essence of advertising; it never grows old or stale, and always succeeds in suckering the best of every generation.

It was a few weeks before the thought occurred to me that despite her overwhelming natural beauty perhaps she was a "loose" woman, as women sometimes refer to each other. I think that women think this reference will promote undesirability in men. Cases studies do not confirm it. Like an old bull to a salt lick there is that constant sometimes fatal attraction to natural affections.

However, by the end of the month, a more fundamental urge emerged. I began again to prefer a woman who did not flirt with other men. I desired a woman who would be loyal to me alone, like Speck my canine friend. You may think that here for sure my optimism is exceptional; you may think that I am severely naïve on this particular issue, but I continue to remain stubbornly that way, even today.

By the month's end it was time for Miss February to move over and let Miss March have the spotlight. I decided not to pursue an affair with Miss March, she was a red head. There was an old Indian proverb in those days concerning red heads—"woman with hair afire burn like hell."

I was ignorant and inexperienced then. I did not know the truth that hair color comes and goes and has nothing to do with it; they all posess the potential to scorch yo hide pretty good. Forget about particulars.

On February twenty-eighth, as I stood google-eyed, gazing longingly one last time at Miss February's lovely features, Mr. David Chambliss walked up behind me and wisely said, "boy, if you don't quit looking at that woman you are going to turn into one."

His words were a revelation to me. He was right. I had nearly done it. I was nearly a hussy, or the more contemporary version of it. In the midst of my infatuation I had lost touch with reality.

At this time in my life, at the mature age of thirteen, my vast experience with women had left me weary and dismayed. All my flings had been frivolous and given me the sensation you get when you reach the end of a tootsie roll pop, and all you have left is a little limp stick. I was tired of fleet footed women who disappeared as quickly as a dollar on Valentine's Day.

I eventually discovered that I have a certain way with women; a way that inspires them to peer deeply and sincerely into my eyes and pat me apologetically on the hand and say, "Terry, you are like a brother to me . . . I hope we can be friends forever."

This devilish tactic has met with unprecedented success in my experience. It has succeeded in canceling any thought of future romance with countless Dixie darlings.

Today, I have a solar system filled with lady friends. They are all like sisters to me. It is historically documented that I have found numerous young women far more interesting than they have found me. Providence alone can explain it. Nevertheless, I came to my senses, and my sanity returned, and I came out of the fog and was able the see clearly again. I hoped desperately that I could recover my manhood quickly.

CHAPTER 9

I decided the quickest way to recover from my love sickness was to return to my cowboy roots. What more manly thing can a man do, except join the Marines? The Marines wouldn't take me; I had flat feet, two cow licks, and an itchy trigger finger. And they were not impressed with a wormy fourteen year old.

I rode along with Mr. Hoke to Quitman to the horse sale to rub elbows with rugged cowboys, the perfect remedy to rejuvenate a withered manhood. Mr. Hoke bought a pair a sorrel mules and a bay gelding he called Smokey. On the way home he began to lecture me concerning this new horse named Smokey.

"Son", he said, "this horse ain't no ordinary horse . . . nobody rides this horse 'til I say so . . . you understand what I'm saying?"

"Yesser", I said, "what is he, wild, or mean, or sick or som'n nuther?"

"He ain't none o' that, mind you, he's just a special horse." Mr. Hoke fired back.

I turned and looked out the back window and studied Smokey a while searching for the piece of the puzzle I had missed. "He don't look like no special horse," I surmised, "looks like a regular 'ol horse to me, just a little taller I reckon."

"Well," says Mr. Hoke, "don't mess around and get yoself fooled boy, how you gonna tell what he is and what he ain't just by lookin'?" Just then, I remembered Sophie and Mr. Gilmer, and I postponed the folly.

"I bet you a chew you don't even know what a thoroughbred is, l'l Keesie?" Mr. Hoke boasted.

"Yesser, I shore do, and you can keep yor chew, I seen them thoroughbreds, seen'em at Kentucky, daddy showed'em to me when we wuz through there last summer goin' up north with a load o' 'maters . . . they wuz all over ever where . . . never seen so many white fences neither . . . ever where you look . . . white fences . . . daddy said it was bluegrass they wuz eatin,' . . . still looked like green to me . . . but we didn't git up close enough to tell fo' shore . . . just seen it from the truck . . . daddy sez them thoroughbreds don't think nothin' 'bout runnin' two miles wide open . . . he said can't nobody but a rich man keep one though . . . how much you dun paid for yors Mr. Hoke?" I inquired.

"Don't you mind 'bout that son . . . ain't nunna yo business what I paid fer'em 'cause you'd be tellin' everybody in town if I told you. What you need to remember is to keep yo hind end off him, you hear what I'm sayin'?" Mr. Hoke warned again.

Mr. Hoke knew his horses and mules, and he knew people inside out. He had me pegged too. I would have told everybody I saw and added some to it. It's hard to keep a secret when a man has so little of his own to brag about.

"Reckon he's broke to ride, ain't he," I asked.

"Yeah, he's broke," replied Mr. Hoke," but he ain't broke like you talkin' 'bout', he's gonna need a right smart more breaking for that. Some race horses don't ever git broke enough for anything but racing, we'll just have to wait and see 'bout that." I turned around and studied Smokey all over again, this time with different eyes, curious eyes, eyes of hope and expectancy.

We got in right before sundown and unloaded the mules, putting them with their own kind and watching to see if they mixed in alright. They got right at home pretty quick.

There was just enough light left to get a better look at Smokey. I tied him off just outside the saddle room, then backed off and gave him a good looking over.

Up close, he was more majestic than I had realized, like true beauty always is close up; when we are honest, and open, and take our eyes off ourselves. He was even taller than I thought at first, and more symmetrical; he looked like dark brown ginger bread, nearly black, hand crafted like chocolate cake, and baked in a slow southern oven.

We put Smokey in with our regular riding horses, and they all sniffed around and snorted a few minutes, but soon became content and befriended one another. I always figured horses are somewhat like people. Most of them get along pretty good, they don't need a lot of government, but once in a while, one will act up and need to be taught to respect the law, usually it's a congressman, but more and more the other two branches are acting up.

I went home and told Denny that Mr. Hoke had bought himself a racehorse. Denny wanted to go see him right then, so we did. He couldn't tell much about him in the dark, but I shed as much light on him as I could, making up stories as they came to me. I told him Smokey was the fastest horse Mr. Hoke had ever seen, maybe even the fastest horse he would ever see. Mr. Hoke never said it just that way, but facts ain't that important to a bragging man.

Denny wanted to ride him, but I told him Mr. Hoke told me "to keep my hind end off him."

Denny said, "he didn't say nothin' 'bout my hind end, did he?

I said, "don't reckon he did", so we decided to let Denny go on and ride him since Mr. Hoke had left a little loophole. I figured I might ride'em too, if he didn't throw Denny over yonder with the mules.

We got us up a rope halter and caught Smokey easy enough. We brought him over to the fence and Denny slithered on gently, bareback. I lead him 'round and 'round cautiously several times to see how a racehorse responds with a wormy little cowboy on board.

He responded like a giant tortoise, a gentle and obedient tortoise. I gave the rope to Denny and he prodded the reluctant turtle relentlessly, round and round carousel-like until we were both convinced the racehorse was an imposter. I was disappointed and held off on my bragging thereafter. We went home with lock jaw and agreed to stay that way.

But soon, we discovered that Smokey was in fact a race horse, just like Mr. Hoke said. You could ride him around all day bareback in a halter, like riding the old grey mare; but once you put a bit in his mouth, you better look out. When he got his racing suit on, racing is all he wanted to do. He went to stomping and pawing and snorting and yearning to start running, and you better be ready.

Mr. Hoke wouldn't let us outdoors with him just yet. He shut the gates on both ends of the barn and created a short, city-block race track, about sixty to seventy yards. Smokey couldn't reach top end speed in that short of distance, but he could create enough G's to suck you right out of the saddle. For several years I had been a regular cowboy, but I had never experienced the acceleration power that Smokey had, if you didn't grab hold of something substantial he would leave you grabbing air.

After a few days on the indoor track, Mr. Hoke loaded us up and took us over behind Mr. Howell's Red and White Grocery Store where there was a large fenced in pasture, where Smokey could really stretch out. I had never ridden a horse that could run so fast for so long. He seemed to never grow tired of running, always full speed. We took turns trying to wear him down, it only wore us down.

After several weeks working with Smokey, he seemed to be buying into our ecclesiastical doctrine which required a time to run, and a time to walk. He, like congregations everywhere, needed this doctrine severely, to balance his spirit. He specifically had to learn that he did not have to run wide open all the time. He was always friendly with other horses, so now we thought it was time for his first trail ride.

It was not his cup of tea. He bounced, and reared, and pawed, twisting himself this way and that, chewing and chomping at the bit the whole time. He was not constructed for trail riding. Neither one of us was a happy camper. My arms grew tired and weary trying to hold him back.

This typical Saturday morning, we rode north up West Railroad Street past the acid plant, where the barbed air stung our lungs, on past the saw mill where its fresh turpentine scent restored and reconciled the damage. We entered then into our customized wonderland, the wooded trail which ran north and south, parallel to the railroad tracks and on and on into eternity, or wherever railroad tracks go. There was an imaginary sign posted at the entrance to this hallowed ground, "No Worries Allowed."

We trekked onward into the wild and adventurous countryside, further and further from the safety and security and responsibility of home, past the Country Club, on to Redman's Curve where we took a right onto Mr. Hand's property, where the cemetery is now.

South bound now, we marched onward, six or more abreast, unashamedly marring the pristine sand of the shaded and shadowy road, making heavy hoof prints in the dense Sahara-like terrain. We pressed onward, in front of his stable, where Mr. Hand's palomino stallion always neighed lonesomely; and pitched a fit to travel with us, running back and forth and snorting.

Bending eastward and passing by the gate of Mr. Fred's mill pond, we considered the past and future adventures that lay beyond it. Only at his invitation were we allowed admittance, usually when his son Bill was home from military school and joined our party.

Hand's Mill Pond had then somewhat of a legacy. It was the resort where my Aunt Mildred and many others were baptized, where mama said it was too snakey and balked, and opted to be baptized later in more sanctified water, where she could see the bottom. Mama always said sister Mildred had a brand of faith different than her own, a bold and courageous faith that could sprint way out ahead of the simple saving kind.

The mill pond had a sufficiency of amenities, including red breasted bream the size of a frying pan, largemouth bass that could pull a ski rope, and an imaginary alligator which never bothered to show himself in my lifetime; but he was always there somewhere supposedly to keep the snake population at a minimum. The covert reptile always did his part to enhance the salvation experience, scaring the hell out the candidates for baptism.

The resort was equipped a rope swing on the dam. That handsome device could propel you outward near a hundred feet for a plunge into the dark and mysterious water, right on top of the alligator. Everybody wanted to swing second, since we were certain the alligator would eat whoever went first. It is a credible principle that I carry with me today and often meditate on it.

In the center of the pond was a wooden raft designed to give refuge and rest to proud swimmers who thought they could swim across the place, but got half way and give out and changed their mind and thanked Jesus for the raft. It was perfectly designed for king of the hill, the foremost of all juvenile games; and we played it incessantly, until we had barely enough energy to swim back to shore.

Eventually, we circled the little brown church where Granddaddy Huey served as a deacon before it went out of business. Presently, it served simultaneously as a haven for those in a heated passion, and for adventurers yearning to connect with haints and ghosts and goblins and spirits from beyond this life. The two opposing groups fought over the place like democrats and republicans, who we all know are unconcerned with anything beyond this life.

Moving westward now in our journey, as was our custom, we stopped a while at Mr. Hand's hay barn in the hilly meadow just east of the country club, where we routinely camped out and roasted wennies and marsh mellows, and told enough lies to publish a newspaper, or run for office. After this brief rest, we double crossed the Dixie Highway and reentered our wooded paradise a mile or so north of the saw mill.

By this time, we had traveled six or seven miles, and I was tired of holding Smokey back, but not as tired as Smokey was of being held back. I decided to let him go all out to the saw mill, before we returned to civilization.

I was determined to get all the juice out of him and settle him down for at least once in my life. I considered it a lofty ambition, but I underestimated its' loftiness, as is my custom. I cautioned my cowboy cohorts that I was about to turn him loose. They heroically responded, "let's go!" So we did.

Off we went, the lot of us, hell bent, twenty-four thunderous hooves pounding the South Georgia clay and hurling it backwards in large chunks. Smokey surged quickly out front, and progressively and effortlessly widened the distance between us, leaving my cowboy buddies in the dust. They were likewise pushing their horses into high gear, stretching and straining, but it was to no avail, they steadily lost ground, as if they were hopelessly rowing against a strong current. It was great fun watching them grow smaller and smaller in my rear view mirror.

There were at least six of us city cowboys who rode regularly, and as I recall, most, if not all, were present that day: my brother Denny, Connell, Randolph, Robert, and his brother Vickie, and maybe a couple more. My memory is not the reservoir it once was.

After a good hard mile of fast and furious adventure which proudly vaulted my imagination into the envied winner's circle, where pretty girls in tight sweaters gather with laurel reefs and kisses, where friends and family shower you with rare and treasured accolades, wisdom beaconed me to rein ol' Smokey in, before our racetrack intersected with the Seaboard Coastline and the excessive movements of Saturday city traffic.

Just up ahead there was a festive congregation, consisting of every strange bird within a twenty mile radius, circling 'round and 'round like vultures, looking for parking places. They were hungry for their own personal adventure, apathetic to yours. They had no appreciation for the spastic heroics of city cowboys.

As Smokey shot past the saw mill like a high powered rifle bullet, the unimagined happened, something that had never happened before, and never since—the chin strap on Smokey's bit snapped; like Popeye, it had stood all it could stand; but unlike Popeye, there was no spinach available for me. Smokey was not in need of spinach.

Metaphorically, the brake line severed and rendered me helpless to control this runaway missile. Smokey's short memory had quickly and sufficiently discarded our trivial ecclesiastical routine and delightfully reverted back to his inherent nature—to run uninhibited and unrestrained— like a bat out of hell.

In essence, I was a passenger whose fate was in the hands of some random, disorganized set of meaningless events; or else I was safely and gently clutched in the hands of an omnipresent God, who held me in higher esteem than I held myself, and had a future plan for me that I could not presently envision.

Like Smokey, I too reverted backwards to my instinctive nature, bypassing time, and entering eternity. I quickly discarded the erudite and imaginative theory of evolution and became a devoutly religious man, crying out to God for forgiveness, resolute in repentance, turning joyfully from my wickedness, as men are sure to do in crisis. That is the way it is with faith, you are invariably called upon to make a hasty decision, at various intervals, without all the facts, and without the benefit of a committee.

Instinctively, there came into my mind some rhythmic words from above, "Where can I go, but to the Lord!" This melody made for an easy decision. Charles Darwin could not help me now; he was dead and could not rise up for the occasion. Neither could Nietzsche, or Mohammed, or Buddha, or any of those boys, their day in and under the sun had come and gone. Jesus was the only one still available, and you better believe that I let Him know that I knew it.

While I was busy hunting down Jesus, Smokey was busy with a more earthly matter—throwing dirt up behind us like four greedy grave robbers. His GPS was roaming for the shortest route to the barn. And he was supremely impatient and meant to get there directly, in time for dinner.

The problem lay two miles ahead, due south, the city of Pelham and its Saturday carnival-like atmosphere stood directly and stubbornly between us and the barn. Up ahead a half mile, I knew that Smokey would have to make his first a decision, and though my opinion was obviously irrelevant, I was severely interested in his route selection.

Suffrage is a wonderful thing, when available, particularly when one candidate has some merit to speak of. But, when neither candidate has much to offer; and the choice is little more than bad over worse, suffrage quickly loses its luster.

Smokey would soon have to exercise his right to vote and merge onto the hard pavement of West Railroad Street, or worse yet, hold his present course and insert himself between the two hard steel rails that ran over six by six timbers packed tightly together with granite rocks and went south on and on into eternity.

I figured if Smokey chose the hard pavement, he may be able to keep his footing, even at full speed, and if we went down, we may be injured, but I believed that we could survive. And, if he took that route, I might even be able to persuade him to go home by way of the ice plant and miss Main Street and all its fanfare. What a refreshing thought it is, when the spirit of optimism rises up ever so faintly in the midst of despair.

Then, I began to figure the alternative, amazed at how much figuring a man can do in so little time, when he puts his mind to it and is not distracted. If Smokey chose the railroad track, he would be more likely to lose his footing and stumble, and if we went down on the hard steel rails and spikes at the break-neck speed we were now traveling, it was likely we would not survive it. This scenario would require the fabrication of two obituaries.

I could not force myself to think what would happen should I hear the terrifying blast from the steel monster that routinely barreled through our little town, taking our southern delights to the Yankees.

I prayed that Smokey would select West Railroad Street. It was not the first or last time that Providence disappointed me. Smokey, bless him for his good traits, was as immature and naive as most voters are, often selecting the worst candidate, rather than the bad one.

Smokey seemed to get his second wind as he shifted from our present dirt track to the steel and granite and creosote timbers, and he settled in comfortably at full speed between the ominous steel rails that began to stare up at me from six feet below, the distance of a freshly dug grave.

It was an eerie and unforgettable sound that succeeded in wedging itself deep within my memory, where thousands of memories have since escaped; the way his hooves violently pounded the cross ties, ironically producing the rhythmic clickity-clack, locomotive-like sound you hear as you wait patiently at an obscure country railroad crossing for a massive, speedy locomotive to pull it's ninety-nine box cars past your five senses.

Having exhausted my long range plans and resources I began to focus my attention on the present. I began to reevaluate, and revise and upgrade my prayer. The idea came to me that my previous prayer was insufficient and inferior and short sighted, that what I needed now was a bodacious prayer that put me in the presence of a miracle, so that my future testimony would carry more weight.

So I took the bull by the horns and prayed brazenly, "Jesus, stop this fool, right now!" . . . It was not the first or last time that Providence disappointed me.

I had long since used up the conventional methods of stopping a runaway outlaw; language, even enhanced with a diversity of powerful emotions and explicative, was useless; physical torture, pulling and jerking violently on the reins, pulling on his ears and mane, slapping him up side the head, even torture that violated the confines of the Geneva Convention; all of it was a mere fleabite to this strong and thoroughly bred animal. A man with the imagination of a butter bean could easily begin to envision the impending disaster.

Finally, a quarter mile from grand central, in the fullness of time, the spark of salvation came unto me in a flash. Instead of pulling both reins together as I had been doing for nearly two miles, I began to pull hard on just one, the right one. I cannot explain where this creative notion originated; I had never been advised or taught to do it; but I was immediately rewarded with success after the two miles of repeated and abject failure; o the joy that comes on the heels of misery. It was then and thereafter that a series of miracles magically unraveled.

Smokey slowed briefly into a gallop and left the dreaded tracks safely, and sure footedly climbed the right bank just before it would have been too steep to safely climb; he crossed Railroad Street in a small window of time when no vehicles were whizzing by; he galloped toward a forty yard grassy shoulder, dotted with date palm trees, the only such spot that existed anywhere along the entire route.

All of this opened up hope to me as if it were a motel marquee blinking "vacancy". I saw a vision of a Tom Bodette-like creature hovering above the gracious oasis beckoning me, saying, "we left the light on for ya."

Previously, I had never intentionally dismounted a horse in a full gallop; I never had a substantial desire to do it before now; nor had I participated in paratrooping in reality; but I had simulated the adventure in my mind many times after watching Audi Murphy and many others do it. Now, it was time to see if those cherished mental images were sufficient. I estimated I had about six seconds left to safely eject.

I quickly grabbed the saddle horn with both hands, swung my right leg over next to my left; scrunching myself up into a tight ball, and wedging my forearms and elbows between the saddle and my ribcage, I was able to support myself, as I carefully and cautiously removed my left foot from the stirrup. This transferred the sole means of my support to my upper body for the few seconds it took to eyeball the terrain ahead and below.

I decided to turn loose and land on my feet and run alongside Smokey heroically. I projected it to be the perfect maneuver to release me from danger and simultaneously entertain the small random crowd who had recently taken some interest and amusement in the novelty. I would wave a pleasant goodbye to Smokey and wish him well, as he continued on his journey without me, as if it was business as usual. That was my plan.

It was a lofty ambition and consistent with the unrepentant little optimist I was in that day. And though this kind of attitude kept me in constant trouble, I do not regret it, for it protected me from the misery of mediocrity that parallels every other alternative.

But, as is my custom, I was overly optimistic; my skinny cowboy legs could not match the speed of the loping thoroughbred, and I hit the ground like a wind mill, teetering forward and sustaining the metaphor for a dozen or so amazingly speedy strides, before

I got top heavy and dived forward into the grassy oasis, skidding into a lengthy belly landing. Consequently, but not intentionally, the windmill antics, followed by the belly landing entertained the little crowd beyond my desire.

But soon, out of the air, there appeared before me a man of unknown origin and name, even unto this day. His face was illuminated with compassion concerning my condition. He was a welcomed Samaritan, amidst the taunts of the laughing vultures that always flock to the least of spectacles, and gawk and poke and prod at the plight of the misfortunate. He expressed his gratitude when he discovered I was unharmed; a relief which seemed to equal my own, though my version of it was impossible for him to equal.

When he saw that my wellbeing was secure, he began to boast of my resourcefulness and bravery. I am not a proud man in public, and do not often compliment myself; but when another man is compelled to do it, I am always able to grin and bear it respectfully. But in this rare case, my greatest honor was that I remained alive.

Eventually, I found out that Smokey made it back to the barn safely, in time for dinner; and miraculously there was no injury or damage to anybody or anything.

I record this historical event as a remembrance for me and my generation who are quickly losing our memories; and also enter it and preserve it for those to whom such things are unknown. As I do so, I am inclined to include a little poem I penned in honor of this and numerous other occasions very similar to it; when I escaped with my life intact for no particularly good reason:

> The Grace of which John Newton sang;
> On which the law and prophets hang;
> That Grace is here for me and you;
> No less Amazing, no less true.

The worst to come out of this episode was that Mr. Hoke more eagerly sought out a buyer for Smokey, and soon found one. In addition, he closed the doors to the barn for a couple of weeks to give us time to consider the anxiety we placed upon him.

But, in just a short while, I grew generally lonesome for horses and specifically lonesome for a horse of my own. I was creeping closer and closer to manhood where independence becomes a dominating compulsion. I decided that I didn't need to ride another man's horse. What I really needed was a horse of my own. This would significantly relieve Mr. Hokes' anxiety and his liability.

I had money now; money saved from the newspaper and theatre business was piling up. My recollection is that I had saved nearly five hundred dollars. It is not that spectacular for it was long before I took a bride.

I still desire to save money today, but I have accumulated dependents who are trained in consumer economics; they believe conversely; that money should be kept in constant circulation to simulate the economy. They were educated in higher institutions than I was, and are more patriotic in economics than I am. I am more congressional, I would rather spend somebody else's money; that is the way to go if you can swing it.

I teamed up with Mr. Hoke again to buy my first horse. We went back to Quitman to the livestock sale where against his advice I invested seventy-five dollars in a slick haired bay gelding with hooves as big as paint buckets. Those who know me know that I am a miser, though they prefer a more abusive noun.

I named my new horse Big Ben. Obviously, his most dominating feature was his size. It took a step ladder to saddle him, and you needed a parachute if you fell off. Another feature that endeared him to my family and the rest of the neighborhood was his gentleness. He had the nature of a little puppy and cherished the cuddles and hugs from all the little ones.

There is a sadness that returns when I remember Big Ben. I only kept him for about six months. That was as long as I could stand the taunts from my cowboy friends. Ben was slow. He had a loping drawl of a gallop and that was all he could do. God bless him, but he was not the kind of horse a cowboy desires. I should have listened to Mr. Hoke.

A cowboy wants a horse that can fly, a horse that can outrun the Seaboard Coast Line locomotive from the saw mill to the city limits sign, a horse that can swim creeks and rivers, jump fences, stop on a dime, and cut and dart; a horse that cuts his teeth on competition and is discontent outside the winner's circle. A horse like Smokey, except more versatile and manageable.

Ben was exceptionally powerful but ran like cold molasses. When I raced Ben, I ate dust. I ate so much dust that I was afraid to swallow a watermelon seed, afraid it would sprout and grow up inside me. I got out run so many times I felt like Balaam's ass.

When I finally loaded Ben up to haul him back to Quitman, I became a low life in the eyes of my family and neighborhood friends; "how can you sell Big Ben," they said, "he is part of the family now!" I became a degraded ingrate, a villain, a criminal, and suffered greatly. I was guilt ridden and lonesome as a leper. I was told to sleep in the barn when I returned.

Mr. Hoke and I had been in Quitman less than an hour when we saw an old man in loose overalls milling around like a lost puppy. He wandered from animal to animal before he eventually arrived at our trailer. He said his old mule had died and he was in need of a new associate.

Mr. Hoke was a master salesman and never missed an opportunity to add another satisfied customer to his list. He said to the old man, "I got plenty of mules back in Pelham, but before you go and buy yoself another mule, this boy here is selling his big bay for a hundred dollars, and ol' Ben here can jerk a hemorrhoid out of any mule I got."

This novel thought seemed to hit the mark and the old man began to walk round and round ol' Ben and to poke and prod. He stared intently into Ben's compassionate eyes. Ben's eyes matched his size, his color, and his complexion—large, dark, and shiny.

Like an old orthodontist he studied Ben's teeth, ooin' and ahin' at the gigantic pristine collection. The old man reached up and gently pulled Ben's ear toward him and stood on his tip toes and whispered an eternal secret. I have wondered for fifty years what he said that made ol' Ben toss his head and chuckle a little.

The old man hollered, "does he pull a wagon", Mr. Hoke replied, "right down main street if you want him to." "Can he pull a plow", the old man inquired, "like a knife through butter", Mr. Hoke quickly responded. "How is he around chullun", the old man desired to know; he said that he had a little granddaughter who always wanted a horse, but all she ever had was a mule. Mr. Hoke said, "Ol' Ben here, he loves chullun better'n sweet feed."

It appeared to me as if a match was being made in Heaven. Ben would never have to race again; he could use his natural talent to pull wagons and plows. I figured that he would be a lot happier with the old man and his granddaughter. I doubted that I could convince my family of it.

Finally, the old man boasted, "I'll give seventy-five fer'em." I was about to run over and get my investment back when Mr. Hoke countered saying, "make it eighty-five and he's yors." The old man reached in the bib of his faded pin striped overalls and pulled out a large Beachnut snuff can. He dug in and came out with four twenties and a five and handed them to Mr. Hoke. Mr. Hoke handed me the four twenties, poked the five in his shirt pocket and said, "boy, looks like we both made a little bit on that deal."

"Yesser," I said reverently, but all that was history in my mind, I was more interested in my new mission. I stuffed the four new twenties into the same pocket that held three more which I hoped would finance the fastest horse on the lot. I began to run from trailer to trailer looking for the closest thing I could find to a thoroughbred. I did not want to eat any more dirt.

After about thirty minutes, I narrowed the field down to two. One was a stocky sorrel gelding with white front stockings. I had a preference for that color and those markings, but I wondered if the sorrel was windy enough. I felt comfortable that he was strong in the first quarter mile, but I was concerned that he was a little too heavily muscled and may run out of gas before he hit the half mile mark. I did not want to eat any more dirt.

The other candidate was a sleek silver dappled mare. I had never seen a horse like her. She was very athletic looking and artistically designed with patches of swirling grey tints and black accents painted over a silver background. Her bold black mane and tail gave distinction to the random, reoccurring patterns. More interestingly, she was Arabian-like, and looked as if she could run like the wind and never grow weary. She had a fire in her eyes that inspired me to think she was a diamond in the rough, that she really could be the champion I was looking for.

The bidding started on the sorrel and soon went past my $140 limit. He sold for $165. Soon the silver dappled mare came before us and the auctioneer started the bids at $100. I pulled on Mr. Hoke's pant leg to assure him this was the horse I wanted to take home with me, but he told me to just hush up and let him handle the business.

Slowly, the bids rose to $125. Mr. Hoke never acknowledged that he was interested in bidding. It worried me the way he casually glanced about the place as if my prize horse had no value whatsoever. The bid lingered at $125 until the auctioneer began to say, "$125 . . . going once, $125 . . . going twice . . ." and just before my heart gave out Mr. Hoke hollered—"$130!" The auctioneer took the bid and asked for $135. A stout cowboy in a straw hat gave it to him. Then he wanted $140 and Mr.

Hoke supplied it. I punched Mr. Hoke on the leg to let him know that I was out of money, but he paid me no mind. A short battle then ensued between Mr. Hoke, the sly mule trader, and the stout cowboy in the straw hat.

The cowboy bided $145, Mr. Hoke $150, the cowboy $155, Mr. Hoke $160, the cowboy $165, Mr. Hoke $170. Then, the cowboy balked. The auctioneer held his finger in the cowboy's face and spurred him to cough up another five dollars. On and on he went pestering, but the cowboy was content and shook his head.

The auctioneer was not content and canvassed the crowd from stem to stern searching for a new buyer. He was as contrary as auctioneers generally are, always wanting more. I held my breath as he lingered forever bellowing . . ."do I hear $175" . . . the assembly grew silent as the auctioneer pleaded for another five dollar bump. Finally, when my wits were fully exhausted he said, "$170 going once . . . $170 going twice . . . sold to the gentleman with the big cigar!"

What a relief it was to boldly speculate that my dirt eating days had come to an end. I reached in my pocket and pulled out seven wadded up twenties and ironed them smooth. I handed them to Mr. Hoke. He folded them, slid them down into his right front pants' pocket and grinned.

There was a powerful message in that grin, the very message inherent in all great relationships. It assured me that he was a man who came through in a pinch, a man to be trusted, and a man who trusted me to repay the thirty dollars of unsolicited credit that he had just extended me. We both knew that without it I could not have bought the horse.

I grinned back, acknowledging my gratitude and guaranteeing repayment. No words were ever spoken thereafter concerning the transaction. The following day I repaid the thirty dollars, but I was aware that I could never repay the patience and trust that Mr. Hoke provided over the years. All of us have those debts we owe that go deeper than economics, those moral and spiritual obligations that can only be repaid by recycling the blessings we have received and passing them on to others.

I accurately predicted the attitude of my friends and family toward my new horse. It was no great feat, most people can do it. You don't need a government study to predict what the vast majority will think or do.

My family and friends did not warm up to Gypsie. They needed time to mourn the loss of ol Ben. But the feeling was mutual; neither did Gypsie warm up to them, or to me.

Lonesomeness has its advantages, if you are able to bear it. Sleeping alone in a barn is not so great an affliction, on a limited basis.

Gypsie was excessively skidish. Perhaps it was the stress of the sale atmosphere, the new faces and strange places that spooked her. Give her a good night's rest and she'll be find I thought. I was wrong. It is a perilous thing to predict the behavior of a stranger.

The next morning, as I stepped into Gypsie's stall, she pinned her ears back and whirled around, giving me only a split second's notice, instinctively I ducked as both back hooves flew violently by my head, splintering the wooden gate and severing it from its hinges. Nearly trampling me, she stampeded through the opening and bolted into the pasture. It was another one of those moments frozen in time when I realized I had cheated death, that Grace is real, that for some particular reason the Hand of Providence had given me another chance.

Now, I was painfully aware that the fire in Gypsie's eyes was more than a competitive passion. There was terror there. Gypsie had a dark side, a deep mystery lurked behind those flashing eyes. I suspected that she had been abused. She had a powerful mistrust of people, perhaps a deep seeded fear, maybe even hatred. Many unanswered questions loomed about. I didn't know her history, but I had been around horses enough to know it was extremely rare for a horse to behave the way she did.

Slowly and gradually over several months, Gypsie began to relax a little, but only around me. She did not like other people or other horses. So, she and I rode alone. I never gave up hope that she would adjust and learn to ride with the group because she was quick and could have run a close second to Smokey. I had accurately predicted that my dirt eating days were over, but because of her violent and unpredictable nature none of my cowboy friends wanted to be around her.

Gypsie's favorite place was the cotton gin, where the rich cotton seed oil spilled into the turf and encouraged it to grow tall and dark and sweet. She seemed to relax more so there than any other place. I would take her there in a halter so the bit would not be worrisome to her as she grazed.

It was shady and peaceful there on the east side where we went everyday just before sun down. I would tie her off and sit in the shade and lean back against the timbers and admire her as she sorted through the foliage for the sweetest smelling clumps.

She was a beautiful animal—angular, sleek, symmetrical, muscular. Her beauty made it easy to forget the flaw that lived within her, but I knew that I could never forget it; it might cost me more than I was willing to pay.

CHAPTER 10

One ordinary evening after supper, as the dusk inched itself in and pressed the daylight back against the western horizon, there came a polite and gentle knock at our back door. It was daddy's mother, the family matriarch. We chullun called her Mom Powell, though occasionally we succumbed to the temptation to call her Duck, like some brave grown-ups would quip from time to time. But, we were quick to temper our smart mouths with a giggle, and run away, before she playfully hit us with her broom. And we always repented before sundown; we still knew what shame was, back in those days.

Mom Powell was about ninety pounds, when she had her old nine pound iron in her hand. She was hardened steel wrapped in a velvet cocoon of compassion. She could stand between a rebellious man and the devil and rebuke them both. She would shame them both too, with no more than her eyes, and send them sulking off in opposite directions, with their tail between their legs. I saw her do it routinely.

We did not know that Mom Powell had been at work for months, praying her way through sleepless nights, searching for answers, as matriarchs often do. Now, she had her answer, and her spirit caressed it, as she carried it a half mile up the alley to our back door. It was not unusual for her to walk a half mile or more, she never learned to drive, never wanted to, never could see over the dashboard.

Three times a week she walked up the sidewalk to church; sometimes with a few young'uns in tow, but mostly by herself. Sitting on the front porch swing on Wednesday nights, watching her disappear behind the azalea bushes, sometimes made me think of an old church song, "though none go with me, I still will follow."

She wore her little grey hat hunkered down tight against her ears, the helmet of salvation it was; and the feather that rode along atop that hat and dangled its feet off the tail gate designated her as the flag bearer for a little Baptist remnant that marched stoically through enemy lines singing "Onward Christian Soldiers."

If it rained she used her parasol as her shield of faith. If it stormed she reluctantly resurrected Daddy Powell and ordained him, and trusted God that he was sober enough to keep his ol' International in the right lane for a few blocks.

If I ever got lonesome for Mom Powell, I knew where to find her; she would be rocking in her bedroom in her tiny chair with its puffy green seat cushion, and a hundred year old plaid shawl draped across legs.

She would be pulled up close, next to the hearth, where once a fire burned softly. She never learned to like the ugly space heater that took her fire's place, and she seemed to silently curse it. I knew that Mon Powell would not curse, even to get her fire back, but in my mind I could envision her sticking her tongue out at the hideous ol' thing that had tried to steal her precious memories.

If she wasn't rocking and humming and meditating, I found her in the kitchen, rattling pots and pans and dishes; back and forth she went from the kitchen to the table, to the cupboard, and on and on in that small and monotonous orbit. And all the while, she would beg over and over to let her get me this or that, eventually naming everything on the menu a dozen times. That was the essence and joy of her life, as I saw it through a little boy's eyes.

I could not remember Mom Powell ever coming to our new house, since we moved out of hers. I wondered what had brought her there now. Mama was as curious as we were as she graciously opened the glass doors to the parlor, doors to the inner sanctuary that never opened to laity. Only the most holy were welcome there in that inner sanctum. Doom and death loomed and lurked there for little delinquents who dared to enter.

We peered anxiously through the glass as mama sat with her mother-in-law in solemn assembly, their hands folded in their laps, their knees gently touching, their eyes intently speculating. Soon mama arose and shooed us away; back to Gunsmoke where our curiosity could grow more passive. Neither my mother nor my grandmother had a taste for lengthy conversation; consequently, the council soon ended, the meeting adjourned and the stained glass doors swung open.

Mom Powell quietly exited as apologetically as she had entered and faded back into the alley shadows without explanation. What had been her mission we wondered? We began to pester mama to unveil it.

Mama gathered us around the kitchen table, the buttermilk table we called it; not because it was white, like buttermilk; but because of the day Philip had taken a big swallow of buttermilk, thinking it was the regular kind, and spit it out all over the little table, christening it thereafter with its new identity.

Mama began to unravel the reason for the mysterious visit. She began retelling what Mom Powell had told her:

"After ya'll moved out, Thomas took to the bottle again. He's gotten worse and worse through the years, and now he can't put it down. When ya'll were there, he only nipped a little now and then, but now it's every day. This evening he hit me in the face and broke my glasses, he has never done that before, I don't think he meant to do it, but he did it anyway. I'm a little scared of him now. The lick'r has taken over, things are out of hand, I can't manage no more by myself. I hope you will consider moving back, maybe he will go back to nipping again, like he used to when we were all there together."

Mom Powell's proposal was short and direct, just as she was. These were dreaded words, troubling words, life changing words, words that caused your heart to sink and stoop and stagger; but they rang true.

Her words revealed what we had postponed believing; what the families' of alcoholics more fully know, that once the door is opened to addiction, once the demon takes up residence in a place, there is no human antidote; the demon of addiction will not rest until he destroys everything and everybody in the house.

We did not know then what we know now, nobody does at the onset. We were all children then, even mama, in the sense that we were all naïve to the danger that lurked behind this brand of evil. We were innocent, dependent, and trusted that the people closest to us would straighten up and fly right and do the right thing. We were sure that it would all soon pass into history and be forgotten, like the mumps and measles.

Mama knew more than Mom Powell, and the rest of us. She knew that Mom Powell's narrative was only half the story; maybe much less; we had some mumps and measles of our own. Mama had a silent war on her own shore which doubled her burden and darkened the forecast.

Since we left the home place my father too had taken up the bottle and begun a battle of his own; and he was losing; the demons that pursued him had grown in quantum leaps in strength and number.

There was no discussion around the little buttermilk table that night, just a somber silence. Nobody said, "I don't want to move back, or vice versa." There was no opinions offered; no suggestions; no revelations; neither was there any whining, or wailing, or complaining; we just stared into mama's hopeful eyes and trusted, and waited patiently, like she had taught us.

Hope quite often ventures out into the wide world looking for a new home. Finding little comfort and shelter in the hearts of dishonest and greedy men, its winds its way back to its birthplace, to the open arms of maternity, where it is always welcomed and loved. Women are superior in this way, the way of restoration and reconciliation. It is an inequality that men cannot understand and often abuse.

We, too often, load our mothers and wives and daughters up with burdens that we alone should bear; and we slowly siphon off the treasured hope they need to carry on. This is perhaps the greatest tragedy in all of mankind, the attempt of men to irresponsibly dump their personally assigned duties into the laps of women. We callously ask them to carry our burdens, and theirs as well .The world we live in today is in deep trouble because of it.

Rarely did any of us ever question our mother's judgment, or her integrity. The few times we did, it transformed us into dunces and reaffirmed her credibility. Over the long haul, as hard headed as I am, I eventually became convinced that she knew best and had my best interest at heart. I knew now that she would make the right decision. She always did.

After I was born, mama wisely meditated, and waited four years for me to mature somewhat before providing me with an accomplice. She toted him home from Dr. Brim's little clinic in October 1950 and named him Dennis. Later, we called him Dennis the Menace, but it was a lie, there was no menace in him, he was much less a nuisance than I was, no colic, no whining, very pleasant in nature, moderate and thoughtful in his behavior, content with his station and status.

Dennis liberated my mother's fear that a second child would be as much trouble as the first. He was very much unlike me, not high strung or high maintenance, his tachometer rarely registered above an idle. He has never changed.

Inspired by the improvement she made from her first child to her second, mama soon revisited Dr. Brim's little clinic and returned with Philip. By then it was February 1952. Again she succeeded. Philip was as content as a cabbage and made me to look like a crabapple. You could hardly notice Philip's presence. He required very little attention. He was devoutly independent. He preferred that you go on about your business and leave him alone.

Making steady improvement in the quality of her offspring, mama wasted little maternal time. In October 1953, she hurried home with a big smile and her first and only daughter, Cheryl she called her. I suggested that she stop now and meditate again and take inventory and let Dr. Brim rest up. I needed some time to break in these three broncos before she overloaded the stalls.

She thought it over and agreed, after the tiny tomboy refused to behave feminine. Mama couldn't duct tape a dress on that little filly. Cheryl shared the bunkhouse with the boys, hung her cowboy hat on the bed post, and wore her cowboy boots to bed. I think she still does. I guess I never really had a little sister in the traditional sense.

Again, mama wisely meditated another four years. Then, when she had caught her breath, she went and got David in July of 1957; David probably remembers the day, he has a memory like a sponge. Mama decided while she was in the mood to go ahead and round it off at an even half dozen. The next year, Spencer joined us in December, and mama wisely slammed the door shut behind him. Finally, mama decided to make do with what she had. I don't think it was Spencer's fault, regardless of what they say.

In summary, from December 1946 to December 1958 mama brought six little sinners smack dab into the midst of this old corrupt and evil world, and she set her sail to teach them all how to live above the stench.

Any parent will tell you what a monumental task it is to keep a single child on the straight and narrow. It requires immeasurable devotion, eternal vigilance, and divine assistance. To monitor six separate and rebellious spirits is nearly impossible, but mama was nearly omniscient and always seemed to manage the impossible better than most.

But now, mama had an even greater problem, a problem she did not deserve, a problem she did not desire, a problem she was untrained to handle; nevertheless, she had it; and she had a decision to make as to what to do about it. The well-being of her family hinged upon the decisions she made.

Her initial decision, the one before her now, was whether it was best to remain in her little home and fight it out alone, or to join forces with her mother-in-law and fight the battle together?

We were quite comfortable in our new place. It was home to us now. It had been five years since daddy had dickered Mr. Herbert Long out of his little asbestos house on Sapp Avenue, a half mile west of where he had spent nearly two decades.

It was a welcomed transition. It was time daddy ventured out on his own. It was past time. The patience of all sequestered parties had worn thinner than the knees of my Wranglers, all of us piled up there in one place like a growing family of squirrels in one little knot hole.

The new address became our first and only house as a family unit, and it was a breath of fresh air, particularly for mama. It declared our independence and gave us a new identity. Mama was happier there, and she began to sing again. Sometimes we would all sing. We were happy mostly because mama was. With a domain completely her own and room for her family to grow spontaneously and naturally, our budding family began to flourish.

Sapp Avenue was a one mile boomerang shaped link that transported you from the dying city park at Church Street to the much alive American Legion dance hall and swimming pool.

Our new house marked the midpoint, dead center in the only curve, a curve that required daddy to park his semi headed east so that the Saturday night patriots would run up under the rear of his trailer and suffer minimum damage, rather than hit the tractor head on and become a statistic.

We routinely entertained the dance hall crowd after a night of partying as they tried to drive under daddy's rig and come out the other side. We watched and listened as they tried with glassy eyes and wobbly knees to wiggle their way through an explanation as to why they could not see something the size of a semi; the same semi they saw on the way to the party, parked in the same place.

This new house consisted internally of five pint sized rooms, a quarter pint bathroom, and more importantly, a little club house out back for us kids. The house looked much larger than it was because it was surrounded by a front, side, and back porch. It even sported an unknown amenity to us, it had a car port.

As I look at it now, it is even smaller than it was then, as everything is; except evil. Life is simpler the further back you go. It is very easy for me to remember when life was so amazingly simple.

We young'uns were turned loose to roam about freely in four of the five rooms. The forbidden room in our new Garden of Eden was mistakenly referred to as the living room. This previously mentioned sanctuary lay pristine and holy, visibly taunting us behind two glass doors, where we often pressed our noses against the panes and peered longingly into the luxurious space, decorated beyond our means, blocking access to the front door, waiting for house guests who rarely arrived.

I detested this so called living room, or parlor if you prefer, as much as Adam detested the forbidden fruit, but unlike Adam

I had no daring accomplice to encourage me, so I remained obedient and stayed out. I learned back then that one way to make a man want something is to tell him he cannot have it.

We all wrestle with disdain against dogmatic impracticalities. It is part of our nature. It may have been unprecedented in Adam's day, but the malady found itself a happy home in our genetic material thereafter, and embedded itself, and has homesteaded there ever since.

Eventually, we accepted the aggravation that surrounded the forbidden room and contemptuously ignored it, and the front door behind it, as if it no longer existed, the way we learn to forget about those things that are far beyond our reach.

We lived mostly in the yard anyway. The duty fell to me, the elder, to teach Denny and Philip and Cheryl the art of digging in the dirt, building roads with bulldozers and dump trucks, transforming the back yard into tunnels and caves, playing army and building forts, shooting BB guns, occasionally shooting each other.

It became my responsibility to teach my siblings the important things about life. Things like, how to bridle a horse so that he don't kick yo brains out; how to throw a baseball so that it will twist and turn left and right, and how to catch it when it hops funny, and to throw it up to yourself and hit it with a bat; and how to throw and kick a football so that it spins in a tight spiral and don't wobble none; and how put your chain back on your bicycle, when it keeps coming off, and how to tighten it up, so it won't come off no more; and how to eat a popsicle slow so it don't freeze your brain and cause seizures; and how to say "yes mam" and "no mam", not only because it's right, but because it's profitable.

We didn't care for the indoors much, except to wash off some of the dirt, slurp chicken noodle soup, eat peanut butter and jelly on light bread, and banana sandwiches floating in mayonnaise, and mayonnaise sandwiches when bananas ran out, washing it down with white milk stuffed full of Hersey's chocolate. We also slept a little indoors now and then as mama hummed us lullabies.

The two bedrooms were on either side of a small bathroom, a small one up front for mama and daddy, and a bigger one on the back of the house for the rest of us. Daddy was hardly ever there. He had bills to pay, and more and more mouths to feed, which to a truck driver meant more time in the road. There were beds pushed sideways against each wall, north, south, east, and west. There was a long row of windows across the back.

In the summer, mama would crack open the windows and turn the attic fan on low. That handsome servant sucked a gentle breeze through the place and hummed dreamy melodies that lured your mind into an alpha mode, and encouraged your imagination to wander aimlessly and pleasantly throughout the night.

It must be somewhat like that in Heaven, where we can drift off into eternal serenity, no straining and striving to overcome adversity, no aches and pains, no debts coming due, no worrying about your children, and their children, no one to tell you what you should have done, or ought to do.

Even so, I think when we are called to Heaven we will probably be like Lot's wife, who wanted just one more look at this ol' evil place. I imagine that when we try to get that last look, God will lovingly intervene; not with a sack of salt, but with a blinding flash of lightning, and a horrendous clap of thunder; and we will repent, and squint our eyes and jump backwards and say, "what was that!" And someone will respond, "I don't know, but it sure was scary!" I believe that is all we will remember of this ol' world; that it was a short and scary thunderous flash.

A few days after Mom Powell's visit, and the subsequent buttermilk table summit, I arrived home from school and mama had it all packed up. I figured it didn't take her but a couple hours; it wasn't that much, just a few dishes, some pots and pans, her box of sewing patterns, some clothes, and the stuff that accumulates in drawers and cabinets. Our family assets have never been in things. Mama said, "son, ya'll go get your toys and drag'em around to the front yard." "Yessum", I said, and I knew then that mama had made her mind, and we were going back; back to Butler Street.

It wasn't long after we got back to the home place before a policeman appeared on the front porch asking for mama. I stood behind her and listened in. He said, "Ms. Powell, Keesie's up at the pool room causing problems . . . he won't let nobody in and nobody out . . . said somebody cheated at poker and owes him money, and nobody's leaving 'til he gets it . . . we don't want to lock him up . . . if you can come and get him . . . we won't have to."

Mama said, "yesser, we'll come up there and get him . . . don't lock him up." Mama knew it took money to get somebody out of jail, and we had been fresh out of money for a couple weeks.

Mama went and told Mom Powell what the policeman said and asked if Daddy Powell might be willing to help out. Mom Powell said, "I'll go, Thomas is half drunk himself, he ain't gone be no help."

Mama hollered to me and said, "son, look out after the young'uns . . . we'll be rite back." Then, she and Mom Powell loaded up in daddy's two—tone, blue and white, fifty-six Ford, and drove off into the night, like Thelma and Louise.

Mama was right, again, they came rite back. Together they dug daddy out of the back seat and stood him up like a sack of shelled corn, his long arms draping over their straining shoulders, his knees like wet noodles.

We chullun began to gawk and wonder and said to one another, "what's wrong with daddy," as we watched the long kept secret parade across our astonished eyes, as if we were seeing a ferris wheel for the first time. We had seen drunks before, many a time; but they were somebody elses' daddy; our daddy didn't get drunk, he was better than that.

I held the screen door open as the three of them staggered up the door steps and indoors in hopes that nobody else saw it all. We were embarrassed about it then; but later, that particular emotion grew cold, and the desire for it evaporated.

I guess it was somewhere along in there that I quit worrying about what people thought. I just happily scratched it off as one less thing to worry about.

We learned later that night the number one requirement for the family members of alcoholics—silence; you keep your mouth shut; it ain't nobody's business, but ours. We all became experts in that regard, holding inside of us the smoldering stick of dynamite that at any moment could explode.

That night, sleep came harder and later than usual. The windows were shut, there was no attic fan to draw in the pleasant heavenly breeze; pleasant dreams were replaced by tossing and turning; there were no lullabies, just soft lonely sobs from my mama's rocking chair; just the mournful sound of a broken heart, a heart so heavy it takes eternity to carry it.

It was always worse at night, that's when worries line up like bill collectors, each one wanting his bill paid first; and guilt marches in, dressed in his fancy, drab suit and opens up his satchel full of regrets, lecturing you, telling you how pitiful you are, and what a sorry excuse for a human being you turned out to be; and if you had been a better person none of this would have ever happened.

It was always worse at night, that's when daddy wanted to line us all up and apologize and make new promises, and ask us to give him another chance so he could show us that he was through with lick'r. He always said he would not get drunk no more, and sometimes he didn't for a few weeks, sometimes longer. He must have quit ten thousand times. After a while, you don't keep count.

It was always worse at night because one by one, he would take us young'uns and hold them up close, so tight we could hardly breathe and go on and on telling all his grandiose plans for our family. For a while, I didn't know any better, I believed it all; all the things he promised; but mama warned us, she told us it was just the lick'r talking, we better not pay it no mind and get our hopes up; still, with the hope only a child can know, we hoped on, and held on, waiting for our real daddy to return and run off this new imposter.

It was always worse at night because he would stumble in wake you up in the middle of the night and tell you all over again what he had already told you. I never hated anything more than these meaningless nighttime apologetics. They were empty promises. I learned to sense when he was coming, and I would slide out of bed and hide underneath. We all did; 'cept mama, she had no where to hide.

One day, as I arrived home from school, mama met on the front porch. She said, "son, you need to go get your horse and take her up to Mr. Hoke's and leave her up there a while." I was overcome with curiosity, particularly with the urgency in mama's voice. I asked why. Mama walked around the side of the house with me and began to explain:

"Your daddy had some of his truck driving friends over to play poker. Right away, Junior saw your horse and wanted to ride her . . . said he grew up riding horses. I told him couldn't nobody ride that horse but you; but that made him want to ride her even more; he said, 'ain't no horse I can't ride.' I kept putting him off, telling him to wait 'til you got home, hoping he would forget about it. They were all getting drunker by the minute and I thought he had forgot about it. Next thing I know, I look out the window, and he's got the bridle and going in there to catch ol' Gypsie. When he opened the gate, she whirled around and kicked him with both hind legs, square in the chest . . . you could hear it in the front room . . . we thought for the longest he was dead. When he finally come to, your daddy said he had to get rid of that horse . . . ain't nobody ought to have a horse that dangerous . . .

said he was going to kill her . . . wanted to shoot her right then . . . wanted to know where the gun was . . . I had already hid the gun a while back and he couldn't find it, but you need to go on and take your horse off for a while and let him cool down."

Gypsie was all railed up, I hadn't seen her that fidgety since I first brought her home. But she was happy to see me and quickly settled down. I was the only comfort see knew, the only one in her life who understood; the only one who cared. Now, daddy said he was going to shoot her, soon as he found his gun.

We saddled up and we went down to the cotton gin, her favorite place, where she could relax and graze, where I could think straight and sort it all out and figure what to do next.

EPILOGUE

For the longest time, almost since the beginning, I entitled this writing, "From Camelot to Camp Lejeune." Toward the end I decided to call it, "Back to Butler Street." But I never could find a suitable cover picture to go with those titles. One look at the cover and you know why I named it what I did.

As I was writing of my days in the theatre business, mama called to tell me that Aunt Mildred had passed away. I thought it was a strange coincidence.

It was Valentine's Day. I could not help but think, "I bet God never got a valentine like that.!"

Soon, I got a call from Aunt Mildred'd daughter, Dale, who asked me to read one of Aunt Mildred's favorite scriptures at her funeral. It was Ecclesiastes 3:1-15. "To everything there is a season, and a time to every purpose under the heaven; a time to be born and a time to die . . ." I am sure you are familiar with the rest of King Solomon's assessment of the importance of timing.

I remembered the last thing that Mildred told me just after she retired around age ninety. She said, "Terry, I just don't fit in no more, this world has gone crazy as hell, I guess it is about time for me to check out."

Aunt Mildred was born and raised in a different world than we know today. Her generation saw more changes than any generation to date. Many of those changes did not meet her approval, and she spoke her mind about it.

I think my generation still has some work to do. We have to speak our mind. We have to work a little harder while we still have the opportunity. We have to preserve and restore the traditional values that are so rapidly slipping away. I believe that we "boomers" are going to rise up and do just that; we haven't thrown in the towel yet, just wait and see . . . tp

ABOUT THE AUTHOR

Terry Powell is a retired teacher, coach, athletic director, and administrator. Except for a brief and rewarding tenure in western North Carolina, he invested his time in the people of southwest Georgia. It is those people, and that culture, that have left him a mountain of cherished memories. He writes now to reminisce, and to help preserve those memories.

CPSIA information can be obtained at www.ICGtesting.com
Printed in the USA
LVOW040536011211

257324LV00001B/7/P